Further Praise for
When Execution Isn't Enough . . .

It takes execution to turn a good strategy into strong performance, and execution only happens when you have great people and a strong culture. In his book *When Execution Isn't Enough*, Claudio Feser describes in a masterful way what it takes to have a team of people and a culture that will drive execution with passion and purpose. A lot has been written on the topic of execution, however Claudio Feser uniquely describes what it takes to win hearts and minds to make it truly happen!

Steven Baert, Head of Human Resources, Novartis AG

When Execution Isn't Enough has helped me to see and understand some key fundamental issues of leadership in real practice and the most efficient and rational ways to address them, based on science and empirical data. The book is a must-have tool kit for anyone who leads others against internal/external challenges for common benefit.

Tserenpuntsag Boldbaatar, Chairman of the Board of Directors, Newcom

Claudio Feser combines brilliantly the art and science of what it takes to inspire and influence people and create positive energy in organizations. This book features great real-life examples and a new influence framework for leaders of 21st century organizations who want to make a difference. All leaders should read this book!

Nick van Dam, PhD, Global Chief Learning Officer, McKinsey & Company; co-author, *You! The Positive Force in Change*

Every leader will recognize himself somewhere in this book. Claudio Feser uses real-life situations and characters to illustrate the process by which leaders can win the hearts and minds of people, and by which they can elevate the performance of their organizations in times of change and transformation. *When Execution Isn't Enough* is an inspiring and thoroughly enjoyable read.

Rolf Dörig, Chairman of the Board of Directors, Adecco and Swiss Life

This book is unputdownable. A page turner that will make those reading it become more emotionally intelligent and better leaders. Claudio Feser has integrated many breakthrough concepts and research and brought them together in a powerful guide to inspiring people and organizations to greatness. A brilliant book!

Patrick Frost, Group CEO, Swiss Life

Like with his last book *Serial Innovators*, Claudio Feser has managed again to write a book that is academically through, utterly practical, entertaining, and inspiring. With his new book *When Execution Isn't Enough*, Claudio draws on a wide range of research to illustrate how to inspire individuals and entire organizations to great performance. Like with his last book, Claudio does so telling a story. It is a story of a company transformation. It is a story of inspiring leadership.

Thomas Gutzwiller, Academic Director at the Henri B. Meier Unternehmerschule, St. Gallen

When Execution Isn't Enough is a great blend of very practical advice and sound conceptual thinking. A truly enjoyable must-read for any executive who is serious about to inspire organizations to great performance.

Axel Lehmann, Group Chief Operating Officer, UBS AG

In this growingly complex world, inspirational leadership represents the only sustainable competitive advantage for business organizations. This book represents a step change in how to look at inspirational leadership, focusing on the neurological and scientific mechanism underpinning it, identifying an effective and pragmatic way forward for leaders. Very powerful for addressing the many dark sides of transformational challenges of most organization. Do not miss it!

Monica Possa, Group HR & Organization Director, Assicurazioni Generali S.p.A.

When Execution Isn't Enough builds on a wide range of research and practical insights to show how to inspire and lead organizations through periods of great challenge and change. An essential guide for anyone leading organizations in today's fast-paced markets.

Kristof Terryn, CEO General Insurance, Zurich Insurance Group

In this thoroughly researched and very practical guide Claudio Feser takes a closer look on what likely constitutes the secret to real and enduring success in most organizations: The executive's competence to motivate others by inspirational leadership.

Bernd Uhe, Head of Human Resources, Banque Pictet & Cie SA

Inspirational leadership is a necessary feature of any energized, and effective organization. In today's fast-changing world, it is arguably the key ingredient that enables businesses to adapt and thrive and to achieve high levels of performance over long periods of time. *When Execution Is Not Enough* discusses the process of inspirational leadership and how these principles can be applied in practice when leading individuals, teams, or even the largest organizations. It is a must-read for anyone responsible for leading an enterprise in today's challenging environment.

Peter Voser, Chairman of the Board, ABB Ltd.

This work draws on a wide set of disciplines—new and old—to shed light on the behavior of leaders in organizations. *When Execution Isn't Enough* is about the key ingredient to building exceptional and enduring organizations: inspiration. A great read for anyone leading organizations through periods of change.

Graham Ward, PhD, Adjunct Professor of Leadership, Leadership Development Practice Director, INSEAD Global Leadership Centre

When Execution Isn't Enough is a rich source of insights for leaders who are leading their organizations through major corporate transformations. It helps leaders become more effective in engaging, energizing, and motivating the people they lead to great performance.

Andre Wyss, President Novartis Operations, Country President for Switzerland, Novartis AG

When Execution Isn't Enough

When Execution Isn't Enough

Decoding Inspirational Leadership

CLAUDIO FESER

Foreword by
MANFRED KETS DE VRIES

WILEY

Copyright © 2016 by McKinsey & Company. All rights reserved.

Published by John Wiley & Sons, Inc., Hoboken, New Jersey.
Published simultaneously in Canada.

For general information on our other products and services or for technical support, please
contact our Customer Care Department within the United States at (800) 762-2974, outside
the United States at (317) 572-3993 or fax (317) 572-4002.

Wiley publishes in a variety of print and electronic formats and by print-on-demand. Some
material included with standard print versions of this book may not be included in e-books or
in print-on-demand. If this book refers to media such as a CD or DVD that is not included in
the version you purchased, you may download this material at http://booksupport.wiley.com.
For more information about Wiley products, visit www.wiley.com.

Library of Congress Cataloging-in-Publication Data:

ISBN 978-1-119-30265-0 (Hardcover)
ISBN 978-1-119-30271-1 (ePDF)
ISBN 978-1-119-30266-7 (ePub)

Printed in the United States of America

10 9 8 7 6 5 4 3 2 1

To Evelyne, Dario, and Alessio

Contents

It has been said that man is a rational animal. All my life I have been searching for evidence which could support this.

—Bertrand Russell

Let me open this foreword by saying that I really enjoyed reading this book. As is often the case, good books help you understand and make you feel understood. Whenever we read a good book, it opens many doors; it stimulates our imagination. In a very clear, understandable way—using a well-written and very realistic case study as red thread—Claudio Feser helps executives understand that there is more to organizations than merely strategy, structure, and systems. Masterfully, he brings the person back into the organization. And given the impact of a firm like McKinsey in creating better places to work, it is such a pleasure to see these important themes about leadership developed by one of its senior partners, in particular the head of its leadership development practice.

At its heart, leadership is about human behavior—what we do, and why we do it. More specifically, leadership is about the way people behave in organizations, and effective leaders are those who understand human behavior. Effective leaders are those who can calm the anxieties of their followers, arouse their hopes, increase their aspirations, energize them, and inspire them to positive action. We should always keep in mind that rational thoughts never drive people the way emotions do.

However, most definitions of leadership, methodologies for studying leadership, and recommendations for leadership development address observable and conscious behaviors. They are restricted to a mechanical view of life in the workplace, and they subscribe to the myth that the only thing that matters is what we see and what is directly measurable. Behind this myth hovers the irrepressible ghost of Frederick Taylor, the premier advocate of scientific management. Many researchers and executives hang on to the mistaken belief that behavior in organizations concerns only observable, rational, conscious, mechanistic, easy-to-understand phenomena. The more elusive psychological processes that take place "below the surface" are often ignored.

Human beings in organizations are not just conscious value- and benefit-maximizing machines, but also people subject to many (often contradictory) wishes, fantasies, conflicts, defensive behaviors, and anxieties—some conscious, others beyond consciousness. Our every-day lives consist of webs of constantly shifting and irrational forces that underlie seemingly "rational" behaviors and choices—and life in organizations is no exception.

Unfortunately, the view that concepts taken from such fields as psychoanalysis or psychotherapy might have a place in the world of work is not a popular one. Historically, many practitioners and researchers have avoided treading in the psychological realm of corporate life, fearing the messy but real-life complexities and the relationships within. The result is that many organizations and people working in them perform well below their potential. They are punch-ing well below their weight.

I have repeatedly put forward the view that to build great organi-zations—organizations in which people realize their full potential—requires leaders to go behind the observable and measurable behaviors. It requires them to understand the dynamics of human behavior. It requires leaders to understand what goes on "below the surface"—the underlying currents and forces of human psychology such as emotions, values, and personalities. In surveying 165 organizations and 370,000 employees, McKinsey & Company has confirmed this view. The research summarized in this book shows that emotionally intelligent and psychologically sensitive leaders are necessary to build organizations with great health—organizations that outperform competitors, organizations that attract great talent, organizations that engage and energize their employees, and organizations that generate exceptional shareholder returns.

The psychodynamic approach to human behavior in organizations helps leaders understand and harness what is happening "below the surface"—the dynamics that are not immediately observable and measurable. This approach acknowledges that people are unique, complex, and paradoxical beings with rich and myriad motivational drivers. The Clinical Paradigm is the framework through which I (and many others) have applied the psychodynamic lens to the study of human behavior in organizations. It makes sense of people's deeper patterns of thoughts and emotions, and it shows how these cognitive and emotional patterns drive observable behaviors in organizations (and beyond).

The Clinical Paradigm is based on four premises.

First, it argues that there is a rationale behind every human act—even those that are apparently irrational. Because that rationale is often elusive—inextricably interwoven with unconscious needs and desires—one has to do "detective work" to tease out hints and clues regarding perplexing behavior. More importantly, finding meaning in seemingly irrational behavior requires emotional intelligence.

Second, it argues that a great deal of mental life—thoughts, feelings, and motives—lies outside of conscious awareness. People are not always aware of what they are doing, much less why they are doing it. Even the most "rational" people have blind spots, and even the "best" people have a shadow side—a side that they do not know, or do not want to know. Moreover, people work to increase their blind spots: they develop defensive structures over time that make them blind not only to their motivation for a certain dysfunctional behavior but also to the behavior itself, even though that behavior may be obvious to everyone else. Accepting the presence of unconscious processes, however, can be liberating, because it helps us understand why we do the things we do and how we might change for the better.

Third, it argues that nothing is more central to a person's identity than the way he or she expresses and regulates emotions. Emotions color experiences with positive and negative connotations, creating preferences. Emotions form the basis for internalizing mental representations of the self and others that guide relationships throughout one's life. Furthermore, emotions serve people in many adaptive and defensive ways, depending on the personal "script" in their inner theater. Experiencing our emotions and those of others enables us to come into greater contact with others (and with ourselves), to find out what they feel (as opposed to what they think), what they like and dislike, and what they want and do not want.

Fourth, it argues that human development is an inter- and intrapersonal process. We are all products of our past, influenced until the day we die by the developmental experiences bestowed on us by our early caregivers. Childhood experiences play a crucial role in personality development, particularly in the way people relate to others. The psychological imprints of primary caregivers—particularly our parents—are so strong that they cause a confusion in time and place, making us act toward others in the present as if they were significant people from the past. Though we are generally unaware of experiencing "transference" reactions—the term given by psychologists to this confusion in time and place—this mismatch between the reality of our present situation and our subconscious scenario may lead to what many may experience as irrational behavior.

This book by Claudio Feser is a practical introduction to many of the concepts that form the fundament of the Clinical Paradigm—an understanding of patterns of thought and emotion, underlying assumptions, values, emotions, personalities. It aims at making leaders more emotionally intelligent and psychologically sensitive. It provides them with easy-to-apply frameworks and tools that can help them to better understand themselves and others, and to harness the power of human behavior in organizations.

However, acquiring higher emotional intelligence—that is, gaining a better understanding of the psychodynamics of human behavior—is never instantaneous. Becoming more psychologically minded and emotionally astute requires time and practice. Reading this book is a very good start, hopefully the beginning of a rewarding journey.

I have devoted my working life to helping people create emotionally intelligent organizations. In making this wish reality I have a dream. It goes as follows: if—as a management professor, consultant, leadership coach, psychotherapist, or psychoanalyst—I can increase the EQ level of the approximately 20 people who are at the helm of an organization at any one time, perhaps I can have a positive effect on the 100,000 or more people for whom they are responsible. I would like to think that I can help make their organizations more effective, and not to forget, more humane. Too many organizations possess "gulag" qualities that prevent people from actualizing their full potential.

This book is a contribution to helping realize this dream. It is a contribution to making organizations healthier, to building organizations where people are authentic and feel truly alive, and to developing leaders who are more reflective and emotionally intelligent.

Exploring the role of psychology and emotion in organizations is not new. Many poets, novelists, and playwrights have done it before. They were the early psychologists. Among the best was Shakespeare with his plays *Macbeth*, *Richard III*, and *King Lear*. On the heath, King Lear asks Gloucester: "How do you see the world?" Gloucester, who is blind, answers: "I see it feelingly."

My hope is that the men and women who run the world's organizations will do the same.

Manfred F. R. Kets de Vries
Distinguished Clinical Professor of Leadership Development
and Organizational Change at
INSEAD, France, Singapore, and Abu Dhabi
Fontainebleau, August 2016

Introduction

"The ability to inspire others is grounded in a set of conscious, intentional, and learnable behaviors."

Some leaders inspire.

Think of Nelson Mandela. He has inspired and mobilized masses, changing South Africa and history. He endured hardship and served as a role model for values such as equality, respect, forgiveness, and justice. Similarly, some leaders transform and build great organizations by role modeling and appealing to people's values, such as when a leader stirs people's sense of pride and their united strength as they undertake an ambitious corporate transformation together.

Think of Steve Jobs. His enthusiasm, energy, and drive were contagious. He "infected" people with his energy and vision, creating excitement and purpose. He built Apple, one of the world's most admired organizations. With Apple's many innovations, Steve Jobs changed the world. Similarly, some leaders are able to create excitement and enthusiasm, thus galvanizing change. They are able to address the emotions of the members of their organizations, and get them to act and to build great organizations. This happens when a company leader galvanizes an organization to change and improve by painting a thrilling and exciting picture of the future, or when a political leader addresses a nation's anger and frustrations and promises a better future in order to win an election and change a nation for the better.

Inspirational leadership addresses people's inner motivators, values, and emotions. It is a key ingredient in building great organizations, and it is the most effective leadership approach when organizations need to massively change and improve. Being inspired creates the energy, the

1

enthusiasm, the commitment, and the persistence people need to transform themselves and their organizations.

However, while executives often talk about and idealize inspirational leadership, actually putting it into action as an approach is rare. Reviews of the usage frequency of all approaches to leading people show that leaders use inspirational leadership methods on only 2 percent of all occasions. Given today's dynamic environment—with ever-changing customer demands, new regulations, and continuous technological innovation—and the high rate at which companies fail to adapt, change, and survive, it is striking that leaders use inspiration so rarely. Why is that?

The short answer: because it is hard. Inspiring people and organizations takes competence, and, for some leaders, confidence.

However, competence and confidence can be built. While some leaders may be better at inspiring than others, the ability to inspire and motivate others isn't an innate trait. The ability to inspire others is grounded in a set of conscious, intentional, and learnable behaviors. It can be built with deliberate practice.[1] You can become a better inspirational leader.

The objective of this short book is to increase your competence and confidence in inspiring others. It is designed to build your ability to inspire and mobilize others—individual people, teams, or entire organizations.

Learning the four essential concepts in this book will give you a "toolbox" for applying inspirational leadership:

1. **What inspirational leadership is**—Inspirational leadership is a process of social influence in which you enlist the support of individuals, teams, and organizations to achieve a common goal.[2] Looking at various influencing strategies, you will learn what inspired leadership is, how to use it, and when it works. As neuroscience shows, inspirational leadership builds on the processes our brain uses to learn and change.
2. **How to inspire others**—You will learn how to identify people's emotions and values, and how to address these values and emotions to inspire them to act.

3. **When to use inspirational leadership**—Inspirational approaches
don't work with everyone. Learn which people will respond and
what strategies to use to get other people—those who are less
susceptible to inspirational appeals—to commit to action and
change. You'll learn when inspirational leadership is—and is
not—the best strategy.
4. **How to implement inspirational leadership at scale**—You can
wield inspirational approaches to influence large groups of people and entire organizations—the key is knowing when and how
to apply this toolbox for maximum effectiveness.

Before we start, let me make three comments.

First, some people react negatively to the concept of influencing
others through inspiration or any other approach. They sometimes
perceive such approaches as acts of manipulation. Instead, think of
inspiring and other social influencing techniques as instruments—
neither good nor bad. A leader can use them to misinform and manipulate others or to get them to do something that may be in the leader's
interest but not in the interest of those being led. A leader can,
however, also use inspiration or other influencing techniques with
integrity, creating action and momentum toward a common goal.

Second, in Chapter 10 we discuss a model called What Are People
Like? (WAPL), a simple framework for "profiling" others and understanding their cognitive and emotional setup. This instrument lays
out a few questions that can help you diagnose what's going on with
someone else. The WAPL model is helpful in understanding the
behavioral inclinations of specific individuals, and the forms of influencing that might do the best job of reaching them. However, this
book does not pretend to present a comprehensive view of human
behavior. Human beings are incredibly complex, and every individual
is unique. The genetic makeup and life experiences that have shaped
a person are unique to that person. It is, therefore, impossible to
"read" an individual's motivations, behaviors, or beliefs accurately.
However, it is possible in a short time frame to develop an educated
and informed hypothesis about someone else's behavioral patterns or
tendencies, and that's the purpose of the model we discuss.

Third, to make the concept of inspirational leadership real and practical, the book illustrates it through the story of a leader of an international health-care corporation called Influ. I would like to emphasize that the story is pure fiction. Any resemblance to any existing persons, firms, or events is purely coincidental.

> Now, let's meet the main character in our story, James Robinson, the CEO of London-based Influ, a major, international health-care corporation.
> As you are, he is about to take a journey.

NOTES

1. The concept of deliberate practice is powerfully described by Geoff Colvin in *Talent is Overrated: What Really Separates World-Class Performers From Everybody Else* (New York: Penguin Books, 2010).
2. M. M. Chemers, "Leadership Research and Theory: A Functional Integration," *Group Dynamics: Theory, Research, and Practice* 4, no. 1 (2000): 27–43.

Inspiring and Influencing

Influ—The Prologue

"You have one year to show that you can grow the company."

James is sitting comfortably in a business-class seat on his flight from London Heathrow to New York JFK. The plane is boarding. Getting through check-in and passport control at Heathrow was a pain. Preboarding at Heathrow is always irritating, and it's been hard for James to get used to waiting in line to pass through a gauntlet of uninterested airline and security personnel.

James, a hard-working, values-driven, conscientious, and intellectually curious guy in his mid-forties, is used to flying business by now, but it took him a while. Before he was appointed CEO of Influ, his fast-track career had taken him to the top of a medium-size US pharmaceuticals company, and he was accustomed to flying private or at least first class.

James has no one to else blame for his seat on the plane. As a small element of his brutal but successful cost-cutting turnaround of Influ, he was the one who introduced the policy that members of top management should fly commercial.

At first, it hadn't looked as if Influ would need a turnaround.

When James joined the company, Influ was an iconic corporation in the diagnostics industry, led by an iconic figure. Carl Exeter, now chairman of the board, was a former Oxford scientist who led the buildup of the company in the 1990s, when affordable

(continued)

(*continued*)

blood diagnostics was a new and growing market. Carl had developed Influ into the undisputed global leader in its industry.

But while celebrated by analysts, the press, and academics—who liked to write case histories about the company's rise to market leadership—Influ was no longer the lighthouse firm everyone believed it was. In the first few months after his arrival, James had to recall a new series of diagnostics devices due to quality problems and he was forced to announce two profit warnings. As a consequence the share price plummeted. As he learned more about the company, James soon realized that Influ was no longer the great firm that he and others had thought. In the years before he came aboard, Influ had lost its edge.

Influ had missed several technological developments in the dynamic diagnostics industry. Many technological innovations and scientific advances—such as molecular markers for diseases, genomics, electronics, and material science—had vastly expanded the scope of new customer solutions. Unfortunately, the opportunity to take advantage of new technologies drew more competitors into the field, greatly enlarging the number of rivals making inroads into Influ's industry. New Asian firms had entered the market, swamping it with inexpensive, easy-to-use diagnostic kits. Influ was losing market share in its traditional markets and it had failed to expand into new geographies, in particular in Asia and Latin America.

In a turbo-charged, agile, and fast-growing industry, Influ was struggling to keep up. It had grown more slowly than its competitors. It had lost market share in all three of its product lines—Blood Diagnostics, Molecular Diagnostics, and Medical Devices—and in most of its markets. Since its infrastructure was designed for growth, and for ever-increasing sales and production volumes, profitability was depressed. Iconic Influ was barely creating any value for its shareholders.

James came to Influ as an outsider in the diagnostics industry. He had made a name for himself by knowing how to react to trouble and turning around his previous company. He knew what he had to do to put Influ back on course. It wasn't that complicated: stop investments, slash the R&D budget, lower costs, reduce head count, sell noncore assets, and reinvest some of the savings in the fast-growing markets the company had missed.

His leadership approach was equally simple: "command and control"—set clear cost-cutting objectives with ambitious key performance indicators (KPIs) for Influ's three business units, Blood Diagnostics, Molecular Diagnostics, and Medical Devices; develop a set of aggressive top-down measures; and ensure decisive follow-through on the plans that he and his team committed to pursuing. He followed a simple recipe: ambitious targets, clear top-down directives, and constant, relentless pressure. The turnaround was tough. He shed assets, cut costs, and laid people off, a lot of people. It was ugly. He also made a number of bold investments in Asia and other emerging markets.

It worked. Although Influ ended up losing 20 percent of its share in its main markets, profits were up, as was the share price. The board, the shareholders, and the press all celebrated James's turnaround performance. Some people described him as the rising star in the industry. The *Financial Times* published an article describing James as the new "whiz-kid of diagnostics," celebrating Influ's turnaround and the role he'd played, much to the satisfaction of his father, a former economics professor at a renowned state university, and his mentor, Carl Exeter, the chairman of Influ's board.

James once felt proud of successfully leading two turnarounds in two different, although related, industries. In the past 12 months, though, his sense of achievement and pride had faded, as had the board's positive feelings about his performance. The market for diagnostics was growing fast, but Influ wasn't. In fact, despite its investments in Asia, Influ wasn't growing at all.

Of course, James had reacted. He had applied his tried-and-tested recipe. He adjusted the performance KPIs of the three

(*continued*)

(*continued*)

business units, focusing them on growth. He made innovation a core KPI, and he asked each division to develop at least one new product per quarter. Further, with the help of his strategy team, he defined a set of aggressive growth initiatives, and then followed up on them with relentless pressure.

But somehow his recipe wasn't working anymore. The business units were not delivering on innovation or implementing the growth initiatives as he had expected. Two of the unit heads were complying with his requests, or rather commands, at least superficially. They were not making progress on implementing the growth initiatives, but they were generating at least some innovation in their divisions, though mostly by repackaging old products into new ones. The third business unit head did not deliver any innovation or growth at all, citing all sorts of excuses, blaming a lack of resources and top personnel, or simply arguing that James's objectives were not realistic.

The three division heads did not agree with James's vision for Influ, which wasn't as much a vision as a push for growth. Even worse, they seemed increasingly disengaged and hostile, a problem widely noticed at lower levels within the organization.

In the meanwhile Influ's Asian competitors continued to make inroads. They began outcompeting Influ in practically all markets, even Europe, where Influ had traditionally been the clear market leader. The financial results for the past year were disappointing, and investment banks were rumored to be talking to Carl about a possible sale of Influ to a smaller competitor, a firm that wasn't even five years old.

At a recent board meeting, Carl expressed his disappointment with Influ's faltering growth. He closed the meeting by telling James, in public, "You have one year to show that you can grow the company." The phrase and its not-so-veiled threat filled James with chagrin and worry.

*   *   *

That admonition echoes in James' mind as he fastens his seat belt for take-off. Carl has always been his mentor and supporter so his disapproval is painful. He realizes he has to think more about how to see Carl's perspective and how to satisfy his ultimatum.

James is so immersed in his thoughts that he doesn't notice the older gentleman who sits down next to him. The man, who looks slightly out of style with his longish beard and expressive face—rather like James imagines an ancient Greek philosopher must have looked—is reading the stapled pages of a paper titled, "Inspire: The Path to Growth."

He catches James's eye, and James can't help but say, "That has an intriguing title."

"Thanks . . . I wrote it. I'm just proofreading it before it goes to press. I have to turn it into a management journal this week in New York."

"I'm James Robinson. I'm the CEO of Influ, the London based health-care company. Growth is important in my job."

"Dr. Marc Jansen. Pleased to meet you."

"Are you a management professor, Marc?"

"Me? No, I'm a psychologist. I research and write about the process of influencing. And, I do a lot of one-on-one work with senior executives."

"Great," says James, "I'm one of those, and I'd love to know what influence has to do with growth. And how I can inspire our people. This is a big issue for us. . . ."

"Well," said Marc, settling back in his seat, "let's talk about that."

*   *   *

Unknowingly, James has started a conversation with a psychologist who is world-renowned for his work on the process of influence. It will turn out to be an illuminating discussion . . . and a long one. By the time James Robinson and Marc Jansen reach New York, they're friends and they've agreed to meet again when they get back home to London.

CHAPTER 2

Inspirational Leadership Matters

"Inspiration is the additional leadership ingredient necessary to build exceptional organizations."

If your actions inspire others to dream more, learn more, do more and become more, you are a leader.

—John Quincy Adams

There are hundreds, if not thousands, of executives, who face leadership challenges similar to the ones James is facing.

Indeed, there is an almost insatiable demand for leadership studies nowadays. In the ever-changing, dynamic, and interconnected world we live in, there is a belief that ever better leaders are needed to steer ever larger and more complex organizations. This demand for leadership studies has created a plethora of books, articles, seminars, conferences, and TED and TED-like talks available to those who want to become better leaders, and to those who develop leaders—CEOs, senior executives, human resources executives, academics, and coaches. As for books on leadership alone, in March of 2016 there were more than 180,000 of them on sale on Amazon.

There is no shortage of advice when it comes to what matters to becoming a better leader: learning to develop a compelling and exciting picture of the future, to act decisively, to delegate, to motivate others, to be a role model, to negotiate effectively, to adapt well to different situations, and so on. Compiling the list of all the advice on how to become a better leader would take ages. And, as some of the advice contradicts some of the other advice, the list would be confusing and utterly unhelpful.

But what matters really?

This is the question we asked ourselves at McKinsey & Company a few years ago. We asked: is there a small set of leadership skills that really drive the performance of leaders and of their organizations?

To answer these questions we undertook a two-year-long research journey. Using our practical experience and searching the relevant academic literature, we defined a comprehensive list of 20 distinctive leadership behaviors often related to strong leadership performance.[1] They are listed in Appendix I. Next, we surveyed 375,000 people from 165 organizations around the world to assess how frequently certain kinds of leadership behaviors are applied within their organizations. Finally, we sorted the companies according to the strength of their organizational health into four groups: four so-called organizational health quartiles. Organizational health measures a number of an organization's health outcomes and management practices (see Appendix II for a description of McKinsey's Organizational Health Index) and is a strong predictor of shareholder returns.[2]

Organizations with poor health (fourth quartile) typically confront stark challenges, such as low levels of innovation, customer losses, low employee morale, loss of talent, and financial distress. On the other side, organizations with great health (first quartile) are typically performing extremely well, innovating in their industry, gaining share in the market, attracting great talent, having engaged and motivated employees, and generating exceptional shareholder returns.

We were interested in identifying leadership behaviors that are almost always present, and those that are more prevalent depending on an organization's state of health. Our analysis yielded what we call a leadership staircase (Figure 2.1).[3]

In the leadership staircase some kinds of behaviors are always essential. We call them the baseline leadership behaviors. They are effective at facilitating group collaboration, demonstrating concern for people, championing desired change, and offering a critical perspective. Shoring these behaviors up serves to keep organizations from sliding into trouble, but in themselves they do not differentiate

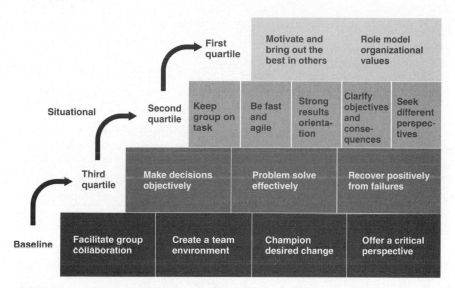

FIGURE 2.1 The Leadership Staircase
Source: M. Bazigos, C. Gagnon, and B. Schaninger, "Leadership in Context," *McKinsey Quarterly* (2016).

between mediocre and top performance. Leaders need competence in additional behaviors to help their organization climb the staircase. We call them situational leadership behaviors.

Our research suggests that in order to move the health of an organization from fourth to third quartile, the most effective forms of situational leadership behaviors are those that are often associated with a directive, "top-down" leadership style: making fact-based decisions, solving problems effectively, and focusing positively on recovery. It appears that those behaviors are most needed when an organization is in dire straits.

In order to move an organization's health further up into the second quartile it appears that leaders should focus on behaviors, which are often referred to as "execution-oriented behaviors": keeping groups on task, being fast and agile, employing strong result orientation, clarifying objectives and consequences, and seeking different perspectives. These execution-oriented behaviors do not substitute for the top-down behaviors that were prevalent in the third quartile. They come on top. The leadership staircase implies that every step builds on the previous one.

Moving farther up the leadership staircase, and building a first quartile organization—an organization that innovates, outperforms its competitors, engages its employees, attracts great talent, and out-performs investors' expectations—requires leaders to add behaviors, which are often described as "inspirational": motivating and bring-ing out the best in people, and modeling organizational values.

This short book focuses on leadership behaviors that build on but also go beyond top-down approaches and great execution. It focuses on the additional leadership ingredient necessary to build exceptional organizations. It focuses on inspirational leadership.

Much has been written about inspirational leadership, and as a consequence there are many definitions of it. In this short book, we define inspirational leadership as a set of *behaviors* that leaders use to appeal to followers' "inner motivators" with the aim of creating commitment *to action and change*, and *empowering* them to act.

In our definition, inspirational leadership has four elements:

One, inspirational leadership is a set of behaviors. Often inspi-rational leadership is described as a state of "being" (being positive, being visionary), with some implicitly assuming that inspirational leadership is an innate trait. However, people lead through actions and behaviors.[4] By defining inspirational leadership as a set of behaviors, we make inspirational leadership a learnable skill—a skill anyone can learn through conscious and intentional actions and con-tinuous practice.

Two, inspirational leadership includes behaviors that address the other people's *true* "inner motivators," *values*, and *emotions*. To exer-cise inspirational leadership, a leader *appeals to values* dear to the members of the organization or *arouses* their *emotions*, or both at the same time. Examples of appealing to the values of others unfold when a lawyer appeals to jurors' sense of justice to get them to decide in his favor, or when a leader of a health-care company appeals to the value of saving people's lives and gets the organization to act. Examples of arousing emotions unfold when a sports coach mobi-lizes teammates (e.g., soccer, rugby) by arousing their anger toward their opponent, or when a political leader addresses the frustration and anxiety of voters to win an election.

Three, inspirational leadership is *goal-oriented*. Inspirational leadership should not only energize your followers, it should also forge their commitment to a course of action.

Four, inspirational leadership includes behaviors that *empower* people, such as setting targets, delegating, making people accountable, or providing feedback. Energizing and directing people through inspiration would be worthless if they were not given the freedom to act on their energy and direction.

The definition of inspirational leadership in this book differs from other commonly used definitions. For instance, *Forbes* magazine has described inspirational leadership as what happens when a leader is optimistic, acts as a role model, displays enthusiasm, or invites participation.[5] While all of those factors have some elements of inspiration, none completely fits our definition of inspirational leadership.

- Being *optimistic* isn't a behavior, but *giving* others a positive, engaging vision of the future is. However, this is a form of inspirational leadership only to the extent that the leader addresses people's values and emotions. For instance, a leader may draw a picture of the future describing the organization as the undisputed leader in its industry, but may fail to inspire employees who joined the company because its mission to make a difference in people's lives matters most to them.

  Further, inspirational leadership doesn't need to be necessarily positive. Arousing "negative" emotions (we discuss negative and positive emotions later in the book) is also a form of inspirational leadership. For instance, a leader may evoke anger toward a competitor or fear of a bankruptcy to energize the organization to change.

- *Being a role model* is also not a behavior. *Role modeling* good values is a form of inspirational leadership, but only if a leader models values that matter to the members of the organization. Role modeling may not work if the values a leader models (his or her values) are disconnected from those values prevalent among the organization's members. For instance, a leader may role model working hard for the company's financial success, but that may fail to inspire employees who value customer service, quality of team interactions, or collaboration more than financial success.

■ Empowering doesn't mean *inviting participation*. As we see later in this book, that's just a consultation. Empowering requires delegating responsibility and making people genuinely accountable for their performance and their results.

Inspiring is one of many forms of social influence. Before we explore inspirational leadership further, let's review the science of social influence and discuss how inspiring compares with other forms of influencing.

NOTES

1. C. Feser, F. Mayol, and R. Srinivasan, "Decoding Leadership: What Really Matters," *McKinsey Quarterly* (2015).
2. A. De Smet, B. Schaninger, and M. Smith, "The Hidden Value of Organizational Health—And How to Capture It," *McKinsey Quarterly* (2014).
3. M. Bazigos, C. Gagnon, and B. Schaninger, "Leadership in Context," *McKinsey Quarterly* (2016).
4. D. S. Derue, J. D. Nahrgang, N. Wellman, and S. E. Humphrey, "Trait and Behavioral Theories of Leadership: An Integration and Meta-analytic Test of their Relative Validity," *Personnel Psychology* 4, no. 1 (2011): 7–52.
5. Carmine Gallo, "The Seven Secrets of Inspiring Leaders," *Forbes* (July 6, 2011).

CHAPTER 3

The Science of Influence

"Inspirational appeals are the most effective influence tactics in getting people to commit to action."

Leadership is influence.

—John C. Maxwell

Influence has long been recognized as an essential element of leadership. A commonly used definition of leadership states that leadership is "a process of social influence in which one person is able to enlist the aid and support of others in the accomplishment of a common task."[1] Influence is a primary social mechanism through which a leader enacts his or her leadership.[2]

Ample literature and research addresses the science of influence. Notably, leaders turn to the theory of influence, based on the principles of reciprocity, commitment, and consistency, social proof, authority, liking, and scarcity, developed by Robert Cialdini,[3] a psychologist at Arizona State University, or to the study of influence tactics by Gary Yukl, a psychologist at the State University of New York at Albany.

In the early 1980s, Kipnis, Schmidt, and Wilkinson initiated one of the main streams of research on influencing behavior.[4] They spearheaded an empirical approach for studying the process of influence by collecting critical incident reports in which people in a work setting described how they "got their way" with someone else in their organization. Leveraging these reports, they developed an instrument called the Profile of Organizational Influence Strategies

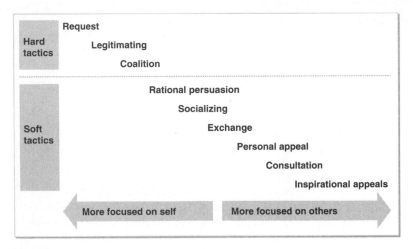

FIGURE 3.1 The Nine Influence Tactics

(POIS)[5] to measure the frequency with which various people within organizations use specific influencing tactics. This original instrument has been used and refined over the last 30 years to provide a solid foundation for our understanding of the influencing behaviors that people actually use in the workplace.[6]

This stream of research has led to the identification of nine influence approaches, that is, inspirational appeals and eight others. Three of them are known as "hard" tactics, and six of them as "soft" tactics. They are shown in Figure 3.1.

The hard tactics on the left are simple and straightforward. Leaders carry them out simply by building on their own perspectives. The soft tactics on the right are more complex and require the ability to influence based on the followers' perspectives, characteristics, and *inner motivators*. We review them in turn.

THE HARD TACTICS

The hard influence approaches are requesting, legitimating, and building coalitions.

Requesting

Requesting is probably the simplest influence approach. Requesting is when the leader uses simple demands to get others to take action. Requesting means gaining the commitment of the people you lead by making a direct statement of what you want and by asserting your position confidently and certainly. Requesting also includes the use of frequent checking and persistent reminders to get people to act. Requesting is the influence approach at the core of "command and control" leadership.

Requesting is in use when a company leader gives orders to a team of direct reports during a turnaround program, when a team leader asks a team member to get something done, or when a sergeant orders a squad of soldiers to attack an enemy's position.

Requesting—often referred to as "pressure tactics" in academic papers—is based on the principle of authority, meaning that people tend to obey authority figures, even if these authorities ask them to perform objectionable acts.[7] The famous Milgram experiments conducted by Yale University psychologist Stanley Milgram in the 1960s explored the principle of authority. These tests demonstrated that people are willing to obey authority figures who instruct them to perform activities that conflict with their personal conscience.[8]

Requesting or command and control tactics may have negative connotations; in fact, people often equate them with being threatened. However, requesting per se is not a negative approach. It is just the simplest way to make a demand in a nonthreatening way, leaving no room for negotiation, but also not suggesting punishment or other consequences.

Typical statements by a leader using requesting are:

- "I want you to inform Jack that . . ."
- "Could you please call Frank and . . . ?"
- "I did ask you to inform him. Have you had a chance to do it?"

Legitimating

Legitimating is slightly more complex than requesting in that a leader adds a legitimation or rationalization for the command and control approach. With legitimating the leader seeks to establish the legitimacy of a request or to state that he or she has the authority to make it.

Legitimating means using authority or credentials to explain and influence, for instance, when leaders show that what they want is consistent with policy, procedure, or company culture. Leaders who refer to management directives, laws, rules, supportive corporate authorities, or recognized experts are legitimating.

Typical statements by a leader using legitimating tactics include:

- "According to policy, all air travel must be . . ."
- "The CEO has asked me to look into . . ."
- "As you know, it is a standard practice that . . ."

Coalition

Coalition is similar to legitimating; however, its standing doesn't come from references to any form of authority. Leaders using this approach enlist other people's help and use their support as a way to get the people they lead to do something.[9] The use of coalition tactics often indicates that leaders are getting others to help them extend influence or reach goals they could not accomplish on their own.

Coalition tactics include creating a network of supporters to extend the leader's power base, building consensus, defining a group position, or creating an "us-versus-them" situation. Leaders who cite the names of their supporters when they make a request are also using this tactic.

Typical statements by a leader using coalition tactics are:

- "Jack and I both think that . . ."
- "Everyone on the finance team says . . ."
- "As a team, we have decided that . . ."
- "Everybody thinks it is a good idea to . . ."

THE SOFT TACTICS

There are six soft approaches to influencing others: rational persuasion, socializing, exchanging, personal appeals, consultation, and inspirational appeals. On a rising scale, they increasingly focus on the people being influenced as the source of energy for carrying out the actions requested.

Rational Persuasion

Rational persuasion is a simple tactic. It combines the request of the pressure approach with logical arguments supporting the request.

With the rational persuasion tactic, leaders use logical arguments and factual evidence to show that a request is feasible and relevant to reaching important objectives.[10] Rational persuasion uses logic, rationale, or evidence to explain or justify a position, and to show that the leader's perspective is the most logical alternative.

To make a case using rational persuasion, leaders rely on having the knowledge or expertise to present facts analytically or they provide charts, graphs, data, statistics, photographs, or other forms of proof.

Typical statements by a leader using rational persuasion tactics are:

- "The company's transformation is necessary to achieve growth, to reduce costs, and to beat the competition."
- "Given the data available, the most logical approach is . . ."
- "I want you to take action. The facts suggest three reasons for moving ahead. . . ."

The logic in rational persuasion is the leader's logic. While the leader adds supporting arguments, rational persuasion is still an approach to influence that—like hard tactics—is articulated top down from the leader's perspective, and not from the ground up.

Socializing

With socializing, leaders start to take an interest in those they are trying to lead.

Socializing uses praise and flattery before or during an attempt to get others to carry out a request or support a proposal.[11] Socializing means establishing a basis for asking, behaving in a warm and cordial manner to influence others to act, being friendly, disclosing personal information, or building a relationship.

It includes building rapport by identifying commonalities, and matching behaviors or conversational pacing. Socializing is based on the principle of liking, which says people are more easily persuaded by those they like.[12]

Typical statements by a leader using socializing tactics are:

- "I am very impressed by what you have achieved. That really shows lots of commitment and dedication. It would be great if you could . . ."
- "I see the problem exactly the same way. . . ."
- "I also have two kids. . . ."

Academic papers sometimes refer to socializing as "ingratiation."

Personal Appeals

Personal appeals are more focused on other people, as they assume some form of relationship and trust between a leader and those being influenced.

With personal appeals the leader asks others to carry out a request or support a proposal out of friendship, or asks for a personal favor before saying what it is.[13] Making a personal appeal means asking based on friendship, loyalty, trust, or a past relationship. Leaders using personal appeals might tell staffers they are counting on their support.

Typical statements by a leader using personal appeals are:

- "You and I go back a long time in this company. I'd really like your help on . . ."
- "I need to ask you for a favor. . . ."
- "Can I count on you guys making . . . ?"

Exchanging

Exchanging is even more focused on others because it assumes that the leader understands what is valuable and important to the people being influenced.

With exchanging, leaders give something of value to the people being led in return for getting something they want. Exchanging is based on the concept of reciprocity, which says people tend to return a favor.[14] The leader offers others something they may want or offers to reciprocate at a later time if the others will do as requested.[15]

Negotiating, bargaining, or trading something, offering something with explicit or implicit expectations of receiving something in return, reciprocating, swapping favors or benefits, creating a win-win or a give-and-take situation, compromising, or making a concession in return for a concession are forms of exchange.

Typical statements by a leader using exchanging tactics are:

- "In return for participating in this employee survey, I will send you the aggregated results."
- "If you support the decision, I will support your request. . . ."

Consultation

Consultation is even more focused on others, because the leader pulls them in and engages them in developing a course of action. With consultation, the leader asks others to suggest improvements or help plan a proposed activity or change that wants or requires their support.[16]

Participative leadership is a form of consultation. Consultation means asking others to help the leader arrive at an acceptable solution, appealing to others' expertise, asking for input, probing for feedback, inviting others to participate or become involved in a process, incorporating others' ideas, or acting on their suggestions to give them a sense of ownership.

Typical statements by a leader using consultation tactics are:

- "My suggestion is that we do XYZ. What would you suggest?"
- "In your opinion, what would be the advantages and disadvantages?"
- "Knowing the industry, do you see a merger as the best choice?"
- "As an expert in this area, do you think that . . . ?"

Inspirational Appeals

Last come inspirational appeals, the core ingredient of inspirational leadership. They are by far the most personal in terms of understanding others' perspectives because they focus on what lies deep in other people's mind-sets: their values and emotions.

Leaders using this tactic appeal to people's values and ideals or seek to arouse their emotions to gain commitment for a request or proposal.[17]

A leader using inspirational appeals might say:

- "Because you care for the development of children, I'd like you to take on the elementary education project."
- "You're the best one to handle this negotiation because you care about being both businesslike and environmentally sensitive."

We discuss the process of inspirational appeals in detail in Chapter 7.

THE FREQUENCY OF USE OF INDIVIDUAL INFLUENCING APPROACHES

Which of the nine influencing approaches do people use most?

Several studies suggest that rational persuasion is the most frequently used influencing approach. For instance, in the early 1990s, Yukl and Falbe analyzed the frequency of influencing approaches by gathering 504 influence-related incidents from 95 evening MBA students at a large state university. The students worked in regular jobs during the day at a variety of large and small private companies and public agencies. Nearly half the students were managers, and most of the rest were nonmanagerial professionals. All incidents were reported from the perspective of the target of an influencing attempt made by a subordinate, peer, or boss.[18]

According to their study, these cases used rational persuasion more than half of the time, followed by simple requesting and personal appeals (each 12 percent of the time). Inspirational appeals

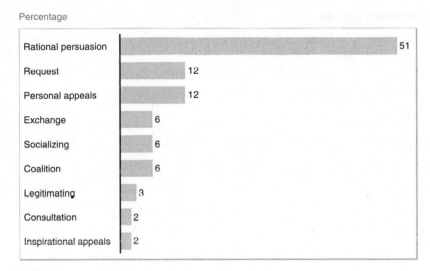

Percentage

Rational persuasion	51
Request	12
Personal appeals	12
Exchange	6
Socializing	6
Coalition	6
Legitimating	3
Consultation	2
Inspirational appeals	2

FIGURE 3.2 Frequency of Influence Tactics
Source: C. M. Falbe and G. Yukl, "Consequences for Managers of Using Single Influence Tactics and Combinations of Tactics," *Academy of Management Journal* 35, no. 3 (1992): 638–652.

and consultation came last; each of them was used only 2 percent of the time (Figure 3.2).

But which approach is the most effective?

WHAT TACTICS WORK WHEN

You can assess the effectiveness of influencing approaches by distinguishing among the three different outcomes of influence: the commitment, compliance, or resistance of those addressed.[19]

- As discussed earlier, *commitment* is when the person targeted by an influence approach agrees internally with an action or a decision. The person is enthusiastic about it and is likely to exercise initiative and demonstrate unusual effort and persistence in order to carry out the request successfully, even when faced with resistance or setbacks.

- *Compliance* is when the targeted person carries out the requested action, but is apathetic about it, rather than enthusiastic. This person makes only a minimal or average effort, does not show any initiative, and is likely to give up if confronted with resistance or setbacks.
- *Resistance* is when the person targeted opposes the requested action and tries to avoid doing it by refusing, arguing, delaying, or seeking to have the request nullified.

Figure 3.3 shows the results of a study performed by Falbe and Yukl.[20]

A recent four-year study involving more than 200,000 respondents by Zenger, Folkman, and Edinger, three leadership consultants, confirms these findings.[21] The three authors found that when leaders

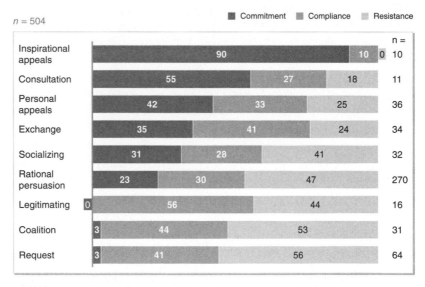

FIGURE 3.3 Outcome of Influencing Tactics
Source: C. M. Falbe and G. Yukl, "Consequences for Managers of Using Single Influence Tactics and Combinations of Tactics," *Academy of Management Journal 35*, no. 3 (1992): 638–652. This study finds that inspirational appeals are the most effective tactics in getting people to commit to actions.

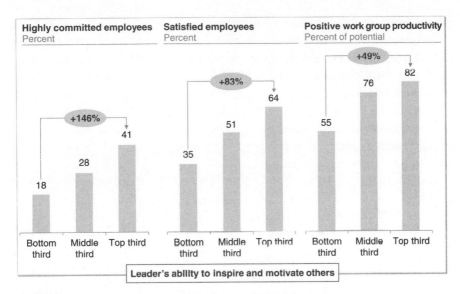

FIGURE 3.4   Inspirational Leaders Have More Committed, Satisfied, and Productive Followers
Source: J. H. Zenger, J. R. Folkman, and S. K. Edinger, *The Inspiring Leader* (New York: McGraw-Hill, 2009).

behave in a truly inspirational manner, their employees are more committed, more satisfied, and more productive than those who follow less inspiring leaders. Specifically, they found that inspirational leaders (defined as leaders with a top one-third score on "ability to inspire and motivate others") have 2.4 times more highly committed followers than noninspirational leaders (defined as leaders with a bottom one-third score on "ability to inspire and motivate others"). Inspirational leaders have also 83 percent more satisfied followers and 49 percent more productive followers than noninspirational leaders (Figure 3.4).

These studies suggest that hard leadership approaches—requesting (command and control), coalition, or legitimating—tend to create no commitment to action and change, or only very little. However, they create a high level of compliance. They lead to others carrying out the requested actions with little enthusiasm, but still carrying them out.

Unlike soft influence approaches that require facts and figures (rational persuasion) or necessitate gaining others' understanding, hard approaches are simple and straightforward. For requests that are easy and routine, like performing a straightforward, short task, and for times when compliance may be the only thing needed to accomplish a leader's objective, hard influencing approaches are effective and efficient in terms of cost and time.

Thus it appears that the correct leadership approach, that is, the right choice of influence tactic, depends on the situation.[22] In a number of situations, hard influence approaches may be more effective and efficient than soft tactics, for example:

- *Static situations*—These are situations of limited change, when the required tasks are routine or standard procedures; hard influence approaches and, in particular, *legitimating* may be the most efficient tactic.
- *Simple, clear tasks*—When there is little ambiguity about a simple task, a straightforward requesting approach is very effective and efficient.
- *Urgency*—When there is time pressure and actions have to happen swiftly, *requesting* and *legitimating* approaches may again be superior to soft approaches that tend to take more time to unfold.
- *Leader's relevant knowledge*—When the leader knows exactly what needs to be done, either because of knowledge or previous experience, *requesting* approaches may work best. For example, a leader who is spearheading a company turnaround, and who has a good understanding of the industry and the organization, and knows exactly what needs to be done (and has, for example, led a similar turnaround before) may want to use *requesting*, that is, command and control approaches.

Compared to hard influence approaches, soft ones are more effective for gaining commitment. But they are less efficient. That means they take more time and effort.

Rational persuasion requires arguments and facts, which may not be readily available. *Socializing* and *personal appeals* require trust, which may take time to build. And, *exchanging, consultation,* and *inspirational appeals* require an understanding of the people the leader is targeting. A leader needs time to think through a situation and put him- or herself in someone else's shoes.

The leader may need to answer several questions in order to decide to deploy *exchanging, consultation,* or *inspirational appeals*: what situational context faces the other people involved? What are they trying to achieve? What background, knowledge, and experiences do they bring to the situation? What do they value? What type of emotions may they be experiencing? Answering these questions takes time and skill.

Furthermore, some of the soft approaches may be hard to apply at scale. You can ask one person or a group of people for a favor, but asking an entire company may not be feasible. The same is true for *socializing* and *exchanging. Consultation* is also time-consuming and hard to scale. It works only when the leader can empower the right employee representatives to agree on a set of actions, and they have the followership to ensure that employees implement those actions.

However, soft tactics are the most effective in these situations:

- *Dynamic environment*—When decisions need to be taken across the organization, not just by a handful of leaders, soft approaches work well since they create widespread commitment and energy in the organization.
- *Complexity*—Soft approaches are more effective for complex tasks, which require extra effort, initiative, and persistence to carry out effectively.
- *Ambiguity*—In situations of ambiguity, when it isn't totally clear to the leader what actions may be needed for success, soft approaches empower people to make decisions at lower levels of the organization, where the necessary information and facts supporting a decision may be available.

*   *   *

Inspirational leadership builds on inspirational appeals. It is probably the most powerful form of leadership, and may well be the only soft approach that is scalable and that allows firms to thrive in situations characterized by ambiguity, complexity, and rapid change.

But why is it so powerful?

The answer may lie in the nature of our brain.

NOTES

1. M. M. Chemers, "Leadership Research and Theory: A Functional Integration," *Group Dynamics: Theory, Research, and Practice* 4, no. 1 (2000): 27–43.
2. K. M. Mullaney, "Leadership Influence Tactics in Project Teams: A Multilevel Social Relations Analysis," (PhD dissertation, Graduate College of the University of Illinois at Urbana-Champaign, 2013).
3. R. B. Cialdini, *Influence: The Psychology of Persuasion* (New York: Quill, 1984).
4. D. Kipnis, S. M. Schmidt, and I. Wilkinson, "Intraorganizational Influence Tactics: Explorations in Getting One's Way," *Journal of Applied Psychology* 65, no. 4 (1980): 440–452.
5. D. Kipnis and S. M. Schmidt, *Profiles of Organizational Influence Strategies* (San Diego: University Associates, 1982).
6. G. Yukl, C. F. Seifert, and C. Chavez. "Validation of the Extended Influence Behavior Questionnaire," *The Leadership Quarterly* 19, no. 5 (2008): 609–621.
7. Cialdini, *Influence*.
8. Stanley Milgram, "Behavioral Study of Obedience," *Journal of Abnormal and Social Psychology* 67, no. 4 (1963): 371–378.
9. Yukl, Seifert, and Chavez, "Validation."
10. Ibid.
11. Ibid.
12. Cialdini, *Influence*.
13. Yukl, Seifert, and Chavez, "Validation."
14. Cialdini, *Influence*.
15. Yukl, Seifert, and Chavez, "Validation."
16. Ibid.
17. Ibid.

18. C. M. Falbe and G. Yukl, "Consequences for Managers of Using Single Influence Tactics and Combinations of Tactics," *Academy of Management Journal* 35, no. 3 (1992): 638–652.
19. Ibid.
20. Ibid.
21. J. H. Zenger, J. R. Folkman, and S. K. Edinger, *The Inspiring Leader* (New York: McGraw-Hill, 2009).
22. P. Hersey and K. Blanchard, *Management of Organizational Behaviour: Utilizing Human Resources* (New York: Prentice Hall, 1982).

CHAPTER 4

The Neuroscience of Inspirational Leadership

"Inspirational leadership is effective because it leverages the very way the brain learns and changes itself."

Lack of patient compliance with doctors' prescriptions is a big issue in medicine. Up to 50 percent of diagnosed hypertension patients fail to take their medication regularly and their condition remains uncontrolled, despite the significant long-term risks. Even worse, 90 percent of people who have had coronary bypasses do not change their unhealthy lifestyles, even though they are fully aware of the risks they run.[1] They know that they need to exercise and to lose weight, and that otherwise they may suffer a stroke or another cardiac incident, and yet they don't follow through. But the matter goes beyond the problem of noncompliance with medical prescriptions. Most of us want to lose weight. We want to look and feel fit. We want to exercise and change our diet. I start a new diet every week on Monday morning. By Tuesday I usually succumb to the sweets in the kitchen, and I say to myself: "I'll start next week."

Why don't people who know that their behavior isn't right make the changes they need, even when changing is clearly and unambiguously in their best interests and comes at a "low cost" (such as taking a pill or exercising)?

In this chapter—and with the help of cognitive neuroscience—we dive deeper into the brain, and into the concept of neuroplasticity, to understand what has to happen for individuals to change. We explore why inspirational leadership is "neurophysiologically" so effective in getting people and organizations to change.

Cognitive neuroscience is an academic field that focuses on understanding mental processes at the neuronal level. It addresses questions of how the brain functions and what biological processes underlie thinking, feeling, and behavior. George Miller coined the actual term "cognitive neuroscience" in the early 1980s. Miller was the founder—together with Jerome Bruner—of the Center of Cognitive Studies at Harvard, and now teaches at Princeton University's Department of Psychology.

Through the use of new imaging technologies such as functional magnetic resonance imaging (fMRI), positron emission tomography (PET), and single–photon-emission-computed tomography (SPECT), over the past decade, cognitive neuroscience has developed an increasing body of findings that link the functioning of the brain with how we think, feel, and behave.

OUR BRAIN

Let's start with a brief introduction to the human brain and a short recap of how neurons (the cells of the nervous system) work. We can derive important insights about *inspirational* leadership from a better understanding of the functioning of the brain, and of the interactions among neurons.

The brain is the center of the nervous system. It monitors and regulates the body's actions and reactions, and is the center of our thinking and feeling. It is an egg-shaped object, weighing roughly 1.5 kg (about 3.3 pounds), with a consistency similar to soft gelatin. Although it represents only 2 percent of body weight, it consumes

20 percent of total body oxygen, and 25 percent of total body energy (glucose, in fact). It has the same general structure as the brains of other vertebrates, but is more than three times as large as the brain of a typical mammal with an equivalent body size, with the vast majority of the difference due to the large size of the human cerebral cortex (more on the cortex later).

If we look at the cross-section of the human brain (Figure 4.1) it becomes clear that it is composed of different areas with different forms and distribution.[2]

Broadly speaking, these different areas also have different functions, which become plain when scientists use imaging technologies to visualize the intensity of activity in different areas or when an area is experimentally or accidentally impaired.

Phineas Gage, a nineteenth-century American railroad worker, offers a well-known example of accidental impairment. During routine rock blasting, the tamping iron he was using was accidentally propelled through his left cheekbone and out of the top of his head. Phineas did not die and, in fact, could speak and walk shortly after

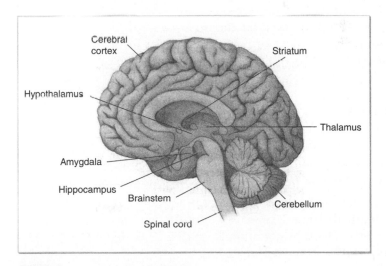

FIGURE 4.1 The Human Brain
Source: C. Feser, *Serial Innovators: Firms That Change the World* (Hoboken, NJ: John Wiley & Sons, 2011).

the mishap. After two months of recovery, he was physically well. But his behavior had changed dramatically. Previously a well-balanced person, Phineas became aggressive, impatient, and capricious. While it was not clear which exact areas of his brain were actually affected, as his doctor put it, "He was no longer Gage."

Let's take a closer look at the broader areas of the brain starting from the center.[3]

The *brainstem*, along with the spinal cord, is involved in a wide variety of sensory functions (vision, hearing, smell, taste, balance), and in managing and regulating fundamental functions of the body (e.g., regulating body temperature, blood pressure, heartbeat, breathing, and digestion). It also manages important reflexes such as coughing or vomiting. A lesion of the brainstem usually leads to coma or death.

Next to the brainstem is the *cerebellum*, which is responsible for the body's balance and posture, and which supports the coordination of body movements, making them fluid and precise. A lesion of the cerebellum, for example, makes movements hesitant and clumsy (ataxia).

If we move further dorsally ("up" on Figure 4.1) and anteriorly ("forward") we encounter the *thalamus* and the *hypothalamus*. The thalamus is involved in relaying sensory information to the higher brain areas, and from there back to the body and to the muscles in particular. The hypothalamus is the central control station responsible for maintaining the status quo of a number of body functions (homeostasis). It controls the sleep/wake cycles, eating and drinking, and the release of hormones.

The activities of the more inner and posterior parts of the brain— the brainstem, the cerebellum, the thalamus, and the hypothalamus— are largely automatic, reflex-like, and unconscious. We do not think consciously that we should breathe. Our brain takes care of this automatically. These parts of the brain are similar to what we find in most other vertebrate animals, and science believes they developed first in the evolution of our species.

As we now move up to higher and more frontal areas, the activities of the brain become gradually more deliberate, more conscious, and more complex.

We are now looking at the *limbic system*, which includes the *amygdala* and, next to it, the *hippocampus*. The amygdala is important for processing the emotions of fear and aggression. It is also involved in memorizing fear-loaded events. The hippocampus is a memory center, responsible for keeping information and facts; it's a critical organ for developing long-term memories. Because we share the limbic system's structure with other animals, this part of the brain is often referred to as the "reptilian brain." It is interesting to note that our limbic system does not mature during our lifetime. When it is stimulated, we basically react like toddlers, even as adults.

Moving more dorsally and anteriorly, we come to the *striatum* (part of the basal ganglia). The striatum is involved in the planning and execution of movements, and in a variety of cognitive processes involving executive function. In particular, the striatum is believed to be part of the memorization or storage of familiar behavior, whether habits, abilities, or skills. Rewards and punishments exert their most important effects within the striatum.[4]

Finally, we reach the *cerebral cortex*, a highly developed and complex part of the brain, large parts of which are still unknown territory for neuroscience. The most recently developed part of the cortex, in evolutionary terms, is the neocortex, made of millions of neurons arranged in layers and connected in intricate ways. This is the outermost part of both the right and left hemispheres. The two hemispheres are sometimes referred to as our computing and our sensing parts of the brain. The left hemisphere of the neocortex is generally associated with higher, reflective, logical, and mathematical thinking. The right hemisphere is generally associated with social, moral, and spiritual sentiments. Attention, awareness, thought, and consciousness all depend on the neocortex.

THE CONCEPT OF NEUROPLASTICITY

Now that we have looked at the different parts of the brain, let's go one level deeper and look briefly at neurons.[5]

The main task of neurons is to transmit electrical signals to each other over long distances. They send these signals by means of an axon, a thin fiber that extends from the neuronal cell body and travels, usually with numerous branches, to other areas of the brain or body. Axons transmit signals to other neurons through junctions called synapses. At the synaptic connections, neurons release neurotransmitters. The two neurotransmitters the brain uses most frequently are glutamate, which is mostly excitatory, and gamma-aminobutyric acid (GABA), which is mostly inhibitory. Other (and popularly well-known) neurotransmitters are serotonin (sometimes called the "happiness transmitter"), histamine (well known to people suffering pollen allergy), or dopamine. Psychoactive drugs such as caffeine, nicotine, cocaine, or fluoxetine (Prozac) act on neurotransmitters and/or their receptors at the synaptic surface.

The scale and complexity of our neuronal system is extremely impressive. Our human brain contains roughly 100 billion neurons, of different shapes and forms, each having on average 5,000 synapses. That makes 500 trillion synapses. At the age of 20, a man has nearly 180,000 km (111,000 miles) and a woman nearly 150,000 km (93,000 miles) of axons in their brains. Considering that the distance from the moon to the earth is roughly 380,000 km (236,000 miles), the size of our neuronal network is mind-boggling.[6]

In contrast to most types of cells in the body, neurons are formed mainly before birth, and the infant brain actually contains more neurons than the adult brain, because some neurons die when they are not used.

Throughout life, neurons remain plastic, that is, they continuously extend new branches and form new synapses. This happens in response to external stimuli, which impinge on the brain via our senses and experiences. This "neuronal plasticity" occurs as initially tentative synapses are retained and "solidified" through "synaptic-plasticity" processes, such as long-term potentiation (LTP). Put simply, long-term potentiation is an enhancement in the strength of signal transmission between two neurons. This is thought to occur as the "receiving neuron" (postsynaptic) progressively accumulates more neurotransmitter receptors and becomes progressively more sensitive to signals from the "emitting neuron" (presynaptic). This ability to modify the "strength" of individual synapses is thought to be fundamental to encoding memories during learning and to "reinforcing" them in the longer term.

In other words, the brain changes or "gets rewired" throughout life. It gets rewired as a result of where it focuses its attention, the insights it develops, and the experiences it has.[7]

People often say that experience results in individuals being wired differently. This is not just an expression; it is literally the way our thoughts, memories, and habits are built into our brain. "People who practice a specialty every day literally think differently, through different sets of connections, than do people who don't practice that specialty," according to the writer David Rock and research psychiatrist Jeffrey Schwartz.[8] For instance, professionals in different functions—finance, operations, legal, research and development, marketing, human resources—see reality differently, think differently, feel differently, and, unsurprisingly, behave differently when confronted with the same situation.

The brain is capable of impressive internal change or plasticity (building new synapses and rewiring) in response to the challenges it faces. In *My Stroke of Insight*, and in her TED talk, neuroanatomist Dr. Jill Bolte Taylor describes her own experience of rebuilding the functions of her cerebral cortex after a severe hemorrhage in 1996 seriously damaged the left side of her brain.[9]

Given that the brain is so "plastic" and shapeable—that is, because it's known that we can rewire our brain when we need to do so (although plasticity decreases with aging)—why is it so difficult for people to change their behavior?

LEARNING AND CHANGE

The answer lies in the nature of the process of learning (building long-term memory), and two connected processes, one that inhibits learning and one that accelerates it.

When we learn, our brain needs signals that say, "This is important. Take note!"

Emotions such as joy, love, sadness, anger, and fear are such signals.[10] For instance, a person may remember (even after decades) almost minute by minute a particular day or event in which something of high (positive or negative) emotional intensity occurred (such as winning the final at an important tennis tournament or being told that a close relative died, or even experiencing an intense public event, such as the Kennedy assassination or the terrorist attacks on September 11, 2001). But the same person may not remember anything that happened in the days before or after that event. In other words, events and experiences that are accompanied by "emotionality" result in more consolidated memories. Further, when learning, our brain strengthens memories in a process of repetition, a process that neurologists call consolidation. Continuous repetition of a thought or a behavior leads the brain to memorize it.[11]

Here is how it works in simple terms: we start learning new skills, habits, and behaviors through attention, a process of reflective thinking, in which new synapses, that is, new neuronal connections, are formed. We have seen that this thinking is broadly "hosted" in the cerebral cortex. Imaging technologies have shown that the reflective system activates the prefrontal cortex in particular. Activities carried out through this part of the brain require attention and concentration, and tend to consume a significant amount of energy (glucose).

Like the working memory of a PC, the prefrontal cortex can hold only a limited amount of information. Therefore, activities that are carried out repetitively to the extent that they become habits (consolidated as strong neuronal connections) are stored and pushed down into our "C-drive," the automatic system. Again, scientists have used imaging technologies to show that an automatic system activates the hippocampus, which is involved in storing memory, as well as the striatum. The striatum is believed to steer habitual activities and procedures that we carry out without energy or effort, or, as we might say, "without much thought."[12]

To illustrate this, let's take a tennis player. The player wants to learn to hit the ball with a top-spin backhand (as Rafael Nadal usually hits the ball). To begin with, playing a top-spin backhand requires a great deal of attention and concentration (and produces much pleasure when hit well!). The player will need to concentrate on footwork, on turning the trunk correctly, on the movement of the arm. In this phase the reflective system is at work. But then, after a player has played the backhand a thousand times, it becomes a routine. The footwork, the right position of the trunk, and the right swing seem to happen as if by magic, without much thinking. This is because it is now stored in the automatic system. Interestingly, you can make a professional player underperform simply by saying to him or her, "Wow, could you explain to me what you just did?" Suddenly the automatic system gets consciously evaluated and loses its automated flawlessness.

As mentioned, emotion plays a key role in learning. The amygdala is essential to this process, as it modulates emotional reactions by triggering the release of different neurotransmitters, which in turn activate other brain areas where memory is stored (e.g., the hippocampus). In response to stressful situations, such as imminent danger, the amygdala can be activated very rapidly (bypassing other areas of the brain) and its actions can replace reflective thinking and learning. When we are in situations of stress or danger, instincts seem to take over (and in fact they do). This phenomenon is also known as "amygdala hijack,"[13] a term coined by Daniel Goleman in his book *Emotional Intelligence*.

In contrast, when the incoming stimulus is familiar, the amygdala is calm and the adjacent hippocampus is capable of learning and memorizing new information.[14]

Let's go back to the tennis player. If we now try to change the backhand stroke again, we will see that the player—whenever under pressure to win a point—will automatically revert to playing the stroke as it has been played a thousand times. The player will not feel comfortable playing the new stroke when under pressure.

The same dynamics occur when leaders confront the people in a company with the stress of an organizational change that requires a change of behavior. Many of the routines in an organization—how people interact, how they work, and the decisions they make—are habits like those typically steered by the striatum. Changing those habits takes a lot of energy, attention, and effort. Under pressure and in situations of stress, people feel uncomfortable, resist change, and revert to more "primal" or "basic" behavior.

Managers sometimes underestimate the feelings of anxiety and fear aroused by a negative change of context, such as news about bankruptcies in your industry, a recession that costs your close friend or relative a job, or the news that your organization is to be restructured. Negatively perceived change creates discomfort and diminishes the brain's ability to learn and to adapt to the new situation.

By contrast, to facilitate learning, use a process that exploits the brain's innate desire to develop, to build new neuronal connections through synapses. More often than not, managers expect employees to change their behavior because they have told them to and given them incentives. However, changing your behavior is an act of learning. When people are empowered to solve problems, when their jobs give them the opportunity to learn (and create synapses) by exposing them to new ideas and stimuli, they meet the perfect conditions to suit the brain's innate plasticity.

When learning occurs under a strong positive emotion (the pleasure of having solved a problem, for instance), that feeling can counteract the consequences of change-induced stress or anxiety and provide the conditions for strengthening neuronal connections and embedding change (and memory) in the brain.

Thus, inspirational leadership, *empowering people* to solve problems and engaging people with *positive (not anxiety- or fear-driven) visions* resonates well with the way our brain functions.

What are the implications of this for leaders?

First, by appealing to values and addressing emotions through painting a positive, meaningful vision, leaders can build a context for change. Rather than painting a doom-and-gloom picture of reality, creating crises ("platforms for change") and anxiety, and articulating why the firm is failing, inspirational leaders can present a convincing, exciting, and engaging picture of the journey ahead. To make the change story appealing, inspirational leaders frame it positively. This helps reduce the stress and the anxiety level, and sets the preconditions for creativity, learning, and change (while keeping the many amygdalae at bay).

Steve Job's turnaround at Apple Computers shows the impact of telling a story that is simple, positive, and emotional. When he returned to the company after a long exile, he reframed the image of Apple from being a marginalized player fighting for a small percentage of market share to being the home of a small, but enviable, elite: the creators who dared to "Think different."[15]

Second, inspirational leaders may want to create the organizational preconditions for people to solve problems and to generate insights from within. Empowering people to take accountability, make decisions, take risks, and organize themselves is important.

One approach to establishing this kind of accountability is to delegate decision-making by organizing the firm in *self-managed units*: divisions, business units, or self-managed teams, often referred to as lean teams. An example of such lean teams, Toyota's Kaizen, has proven to be a good vehicle for creating the conditions for continuous learning and improvement. And, it turns out to be more innovative and more adaptive than other forms of organization. This is reflected in the recent rise of lean management techniques—in essence the application of the Kaizen approach to other industries—and in their use with functions other than manufacturing.

*   *   *

Inspirational leadership is a powerful approach to getting individuals and organizations to change. It causes change because it addresses the process of how people learn and change at the "neurological" level.

Let's now explore how to use the approach of inspirational leadership in more detail.

But before we do so, let's check in with James at Influ.

NOTES

1. A. Deutschman, "Change or Die. New Insights from Psychology and Neuroscience," *Fast Company* (2005).
2. C. Feser, *Serial Innovators. Firms That Change the World* (Hoboken, NJ: Wiley & Sons, 2011).
3. D. H. Pink, *A Whole Mind* (New York: Riverhead Books, 2006); D. J. Linden, *The Accidental Mind. How Brain Evolution Has Given Us Love, Memory, Dreams and God* (Cambridge, MA: Harvard University Press, 2007); R. D. Precht, *Wer bin Ich, und wenn ja wie viele? Eine Philosophische Reise* (Munich: Wilhelm Goldmann Verlag, 2007).
4. D. Rock and J. Schwartz, "The Neuroscience of Leadership," *Strategy + Business* 43 (Summer 2006); Linden, *Accidental Mind*.

5. Linden, *Accidental Mind*.
6. Ibid.
7. Ibid.
8. Rock and Schwartz, "Neuroscience of Leadership."
9. J. Bolte Taylor, *My Stroke of Insight* (London: Hodder & Stoughton, 2008).
10. Linden, *Accidental Mind*.
11. B. Oakley, "Learning How to Learn." TEDx speech published on August 5, 2014.
12. Rock and Schwartz, "Neuroscience of Leadership"; Linden, *Accidental Mind*.
13. D. Goleman, *Emotional Intelligence: Why It Can Matter More Than IQ*, 10th Anniversary Edition (New York: Bantam Books, 2005).
14. Rock and Schwartz, "Neuroscience of Leadership"; Bolte Taylor, *My Stroke of Insight*.
15. Deutschman, "Change or Die."

CHAPTER 5

Influ—The Consultations

By the time James catches his taxi from JFK into Manhattan, his conversation with Marc Jansen has already helped him reach some tough conclusions. He is slowly and reluctantly starting to realize that his leadership approach—setting ambitious targets and applying relentless pressure—will not be effective in bringing Influ back onto a growth trajectory. He hasn't digested yet what that will mean in terms of his future actions, but he's aware that tough changes lie ahead.

He understands that using hard influencing approaches works for tasks that are rather straightforward. Turning Influ around was relatively straightforward. He had done it before and he could do it again; he knew what it took. He could lead from the top, be directive, and apply pressure to make people carry out his requests.

But getting Influ back onto a steady pattern of growth wasn't going to be all that straightforward.

Smaller and nimbler firms are beating Influ's largest business unit, Blood Diagnostics. Its rivals enjoy the advantage of superior, innovative products and more cost-effective business models. These smaller, more agile Asian firms, which first entered blood diagnostics as lower-priced, lower-quality competitors, are now bringing ever-better high-quality products to the market.

(continued)

(*continued*)

Quentin Sloan, the head of the Blood Diagnostics business unit, didn't see this coming. Ambitious and competitive, he ridiculed and underestimated these competitors, and his business unit is now struggling to keep up with their momentum and rapid innovation. James knows that Quentin has strong leadership skills, but he's cocky and sometimes a little hard to like. While the board of directors is swayed by Quentin's confidence and knowledge, he is confrontational, particularly when he's pressed, and he's not yet seasoned at competing in a fast-moving, international arena. To the good, he's ambitious, smart, and driven, but being behind in his field is frustrating him and throwing him off his game, and this may be part of the problem of turning around the Blood Diagnostics business unit.

But Influ's other two, smaller business units are also in trouble.

The Molecular Diagnostics unit, Influ's youngest division, is competing in the most scientifically based, innovative, and lucrative parts of the diagnostic market. It faces strong competition from US-based players who are outspending Influ on research and development. The competition is pouring huge sums into R&D and developing new tests for identifying disease variations in patients. The molecular diagnostics market is "hot," with large pharmaceutical companies and venture-capital firms investing millions to stay ahead.

And that leads James' thoughts to Mary Kempel, the leader of the Molecular Diagnostics business unit. He thinks she isn't trying as hard as the other two division heads, and she's been complaining vociferously about Influ's underinvestment in her field for two years. James recognizes that she might be right, but the issue isn't just funding anymore. Her division is having trouble attracting and retaining good research scientists, and Influ has lost credibility with its investors in this highly dynamic field. Mary, a PhD stem cell researcher in her forties, knows these experts personally. She grew up eating and drinking advanced science; her mother was a professor and her father was a Nobel Prize–winning biologist. She has a world-changing sense of purpose, but she can't get out of the gate until Influ's willingness to invest in its goals catches up with her heartfelt urgency about rebuilding her unit's scientific team. James fears that Mary is already disengaged from Influ and looking for her next job.

The third business unit, Medical Devices, has a product-quality problem. Jorg Morten, the unit head, fulfilled Influ's budget-cut directives by underinvesting in machinery and, thus, technical capabilities. Quality issues, product recalls, and the departures of good people increasingly plague his unit. Jorg is probably James' best friend on the executive committee, but the lanky and laconic engineer resents the budget cuts in his unit and he quietly disapproves of James' command and control approach. Jorg, a conscientious, steady, and efficient German in his mid-fifties, knows what he's doing and is frustrated that the company hasn't given him resources to go all out. Still, he's a reliable, likeable ally. James trusts his support, even if it's given as a personal favor, and would like to counter his disillusionment.

The three business unit heads face complex issues. Addressing them will require creativity, willingness to take risks, significant effort, persistence, and a great deal of attention to detail.

James is beginning to understand that he can't lead from the top with a power-heavy approach as he did during the turnaround. Even if leading with an autocratic hand were possible in James' current situation, it would require a scientific background and a deep understanding of the intricacies of each business unit. James doesn't have either. To achieve corporate growth, he has to trust and reengage the business unit heads. James realizes he's going to have to learn more about how real influence works, beginning with Quentin, Mary, and Jorg, his three most crucial leaders.

(continued)

(continued)

James hopes to reengage Quentin Sloan, Mary Kempel, and Jorg Morten with the help of another member of the executive committee, Jane Cunningham, his steady, practical CFO. He works with Jane almost daily, and appreciates her common sense and business knowledge.

At the office, James tells Jane about Dr. Jansen, explaining that he's learned that the most powerful influencing tactic for building people's commitment to complex tasks is an inspirational appeal. However, he knows inspiration isn't his gift. No one has ever described him as an inspirational leader. James approaches challenges as a numbers guy, a hard-nosed turnaround manager who knows how to lead decisively from the top. Other people's values and emotions have never really interested him, at least not at work. He's always felt that business isn't a place for "soft stuff" like feelings. Business is about numbers, making decisions, and money.

He hopes he and Jane can find a new way—enlightened by his fresh knowledge—to change Influ's organizational culture as well as its business results.

The change in James' attitude as part of his ongoing conversations with Marc Jansen has been slow and not simple. He's worked through most of it with his wife Joanne, finding that her understanding creates a safe place for him to process new information and personal change.

In the past, his usual commanding approach also has stirred up issues and resentment with Liz, their teenage daughter, so he and Joanne have spent hours discussing how this fresh approach might affect the way they are raising Liz and her little brother, Max. So far, James hasn't been able to bridge Liz's adolescent diffidence. He's hesitant to appear to be lowering his standards for her schoolwork and behavior even if that might soften her abrasive defensiveness. Max is a lot easier. Kick the soccer ball around a bit, ask him about playing with his classmates, and the little guy is fine. Max's levelheaded nature, James thinks, must be an inheritance from Joanne. He sees a lot of himself in Liz's tense abrasiveness, not that such an insight makes relating to his teenaged daughter any less complicated.

Marc Jansen has talked to James about other soft influencing approaches—strategies that would probably be more effective at home and in the current situation at Influ than his pure command and control approach. But James knows he has to get more comfortable with the idea to deploy it effectively. Along the same lines, Joanne has urged him to reach out to their daughter, but he finds that Liz's maddening self-absorption triggers every autocratic impulse in his still-limited emotional toolbox.

* * *

One late evening at home, as James is sitting in the den reflecting on how to reengage his team, he sees someone coming downstairs, Liz in a rumpled T-shirt, her hair tousled, clearly sleepless.

James starts one of those typical conversations with Liz, although now trying to use a softer approach.

"What's wrong, Lizzy?" he asks her.

"You wouldn't understand," she replies sulkily. "And call me Elizabeth. I'm just getting some tea."

Instead of shrugging her off, attitude and all, as he might have usually done, James hauls himself up out of the couch and follows her into the kitchen. "Can't sleep?" he asks, "Me neither. Business stuff. What's up with you?"

"Never mind," she says, "you really wouldn't get it."

"Maybe not," he says, adding, "but I'd try."

"Really, Pops?" Elizabeth asks, almost snidely, piling a heaping spoonful of sugar into her cup. "That's new. . . ."

"I guess so. . . . You and I may both need to do a few things in new ways," he says half to himself and half to her, "but it's late now. If Mum or I can help you out, you know we will."

(continued)

(*continued*)

"It's just school shit," she mumbles diffidently, brushing by him with her cup in her hand, wondering if bad language would get a rise out of her uptight father.

James is irritated. However, he almost unconsciously decides not to start up with her. He says to her disappearing back, "For now, get some sleep, Lizzy . . . but let's try to talk."

* * *

At work, James is beginning to think that, perhaps, he can combine soft approaches with his familiar command and control tactics. He believes that complementing his autocratic approach with elements of consultation could create more energy and commitment in the organization, but ultimately he does not feel comfortable delegating too much power. As he sees it, he's willing to confer but not to give anything away.

He wants to retain tight control over major strategic and investment decisions, and priority directives. After all, ultimately his neck is on the line if he doesn't deliver results to the board and the shareholders. Yet, at the same time, James knows he needs to channel Quentin's energies, reengage Mary, and give Jorg some encouragement in order to lead them to accomplish Influ's goals.

With the help of Jane and her staff, James develops a draft of a new group strategy that envisages increased investments in R&D and improved quality in all three major divisions, but also sets even more ambitious growth targets. He starts a process of involving the unit heads. He wants them to participate in the finalization of the strategy.

Ready to consult, if not to either delegate or inspire, he sets up a series of one-on-one discussions with each of the business unit heads, and plans a final full executive meeting (including Jane, the three unit heads, and himself) to sign off officially on the new strategy.

The one-on-one discussions with Quentin about Blood Diagnostics go reasonably well. Quentin has been part of the team working on building his division for a relatively long time, given his youth. He knows his business inside out, and most people in the organization consider him to be a real expert in blood diagnostics. James appeals to Quentin's expertise by respecting his input about Blood Diagnostic's role in the corporation's strategy, but also by asking him for his thoughts about the strategies for the other two business units. James probes for feedback, incorporates Quentin's ideas, and invites him to work with Jane in detailing and finalizing the overall strategy. Having never been much involved in the corporate strategy process beyond his own unit, Quentin is flattered that James is asking him to contribute.

Over the next few days, Quentin shifts from an earlier line of thinking—wondering if he's too young for the board's succession discussions to land on him if James can't get Influ to grow (and if he's on their list)—to figuring out how to accomplish what he now sees as his and James' mutual goals for Blood Diagnostics and the entire corporation. Quentin feels committed to the new plan, even though it assumes significantly increased growth rates and market share gains in his division. He's pleased that James finally is talking to him as an equal.

* * *

James' one-on-one discussions with Mary about the Molecular Diagnostics unit are more difficult. While she appreciates James's willingness to increase investment levels, she does not want to commit to higher targets. She argues that getting Molecular Diagnostics to grow again will take longer than other divisions might require because recent events have blunted its scientific edge. As if James didn't already know, she explains that since Influ has lost much of its status among scientists in the dynamic trendy molecular diagnostics market, first it has to regain its rep-

(continued)

(*continued*)

utation as an attractive place for scientists to work and conduct research. She outlines a frustrating cycle: to rebuild its position in the industry, Influ first must recruit and hire highly respected scientists, and in order to hire top scientists, it must regain some of its lost status—and she says that finding how to break that logjam will take time. Only when James offers his personal time, connections, and help in recruiting a number of renowned scientists, and revises her division's growth targets down slightly, does Mary commit, in return, to supporting his new plan.

What James doesn't know is that she has an offer brewing from a big American pharma competitor, and her concurrence with James' plans is based more on not wanting to uproot her family than on having a lot of residual faith in Influ. Yet, she is pleased to find that James' attitude has shifted from being almost arrogantly autocratic to at least making an effort at real consultation. As she sits down in her office after their meeting, she decides it's worth another try. Turning to her computer, she opens her wish list of the scientists she wants to recruit and starts thinking again how to target her prospects, one by one.

*   *   *

James' one-on-one discussions with Jorg about the Medical Devices business unit are the hardest and most contentious, perhaps because the two friends are less guarded with each other than James is with the other unit heads. When James first tries to look ahead, Jorg clearly reiterates his resentment about the previous years' budget cuts, which, in his view, caused the current quality problems. His condescending "I told you so" statements irritate James, but he doesn't want to pick a fight and lose time—and a strong ally—by replacing Jorg. Not only is Jorg an effective manager, but also James really likes him. They have a good rapport and a level of trust. James sees Jorg as probably his only friend on the executive committee. After two long discussions, which allow Jorg to vent all his concerns about the new plan, James asks for his support as a personal favor.

On that basis, Jorg can hardly refuse. He finally agrees to commit to the new plan, even though it requires his unit to resolve its quality problems in record time. He is mollified by James' personal appeal and financial commitment to his division. And he, too, wants to maintain their friendship—as long as James treats him like a peer, not just outside of the office—where they've enjoyed several dinner and theater evenings with their wives over time, but inside as well. That split was getting old, as Jorg told his second wife, Ilsa, after the couples' last outing. "He's young," Ilsa had reminded him, "but he's smart, and you're very important to him. Give him time."

*   *   *

After all the individual consultation meetings, James convenes a meeting with the entire Influ executive committee with Jane Cunningham to finalize the new strategy. The mood is good, and James feels that the entire top team is now committed to making the new strategy happen.

In fact, over time, the leadership team's improved commitment seems to affect the rest of the organization, as evidenced by the results of an employee engagement survey. Things start to change for the better. Influ makes its planned investments in people, R&D, and infrastructure, and the first signs from the commercial side look good. Sales improve, and after only six months, the company starts to show signs of growth.

Influ isn't out of the woods yet, and everyone still has a lot to do, but the board now seems to be increasingly convinced that the company is on the right track to growth. Carl's support is rather lukewarm and he seems to take a "wait and see" position, but the board overall seems increasingly satisfied.

(continued)

(continued)

James is cautiously confident about the outlook for the future. He tells Marc Jansen that the consultation process has worked well and the members of the top team seem engaged and committed overall.

James feels he is in the process of regaining the board's trust.

Two

Inspiring Others

CHAPTER 6

Influ—"I hate school"

"I hate school."

James is sitting in the living room Sunday evening reading a report Marc has given him, which discusses the concept of empathy.

The weekend went well. The family went out for ice cream together. Joanne had told James that Liz seemed down to her most of the weekend, but Joanne wasn't sure why and James knew he didn't have a clue.

Still, he remembered what his wife had said when Liz walked through the living room.

"You okay, Lizzy?" he asked, looking up from the papers.

"Call me Elizabeth," she says, irked almost by rote. "I'm alright I guess. I just don't want to go to school tomorrow. School sucks. I hate it!"

"Hmmm . . . when I grew up school sucked, too. I never liked to go. I hated it, too. I really understand," James responds, hoping that sharing his feelings will cheer her up and that he's being as empathetic as he can.

"Yeah. . . . But I really hate it."

"I hear you . . . but life can be tough. I hate to go to work sometimes . . . but, look, sweetie, your education is really important. Why don't you stay home tomorrow and relax, and go back to school on Tuesday?"

(continued)

(*continued*)

"Yes, but . . ." she starts to say something, and stops again.

"Listen, vacation is just six weeks away," James adds, not realizing he's cut her off. "Hang in there and we'll leave for Switzerland soon enough. I think it's time to get you new skis. You're getting too tall for your old pair. We'll have a great time, I promise!"

"Whatever," Liz says, "you'll never get it."

Having had the last word, she slouches into the den where James sees her plop down onto the couch next to Max who's watching TV. As she takes a handful of crisps from the bag on Max's lap, James looks back down at his papers.

He's puzzled. He tried that empathy thing, but he doesn't think he got very far or helped his daughter much. He wonders what's going on with Liz. Why is she acting this way? It's not rational. School is important. Doesn't she want a good future?

He turns back to Marc's reports.

CHAPTER 7

How to Inspire

"The first step in inspiring others is to connect with their inner motivators—their values and emotions."

If you were born with the ability to change someone's perspective or emotions, never waste that gift. It is one of the most powerful gifts God can give—the ability to influence.

—Shannon L. Alder

Later in the book we discuss how human behavior is influenced by a number of factors: context, know-how, skills, and mind-sets. The latter includes values, personality, and emotions.

In this chapter, we focus on values and emotions, exploring how to inspire others by addressing those "inner motivators." We discuss how to inspire by appealing to values and by arousing emotions.

To structure the discussion, we can think of a framework in which behaviors are driven by inner motivators (values and emotions), which in turn are driven by the factors shown in Figure 7.1.

For instance, Mary is not making progress with the turnaround of her business unit. She is delaying decisions and not addressing the issues at hand in a forceful manner (behaviors). The reason is that she is frustrated with Influ and James. She feels alone and let down (emotion). The reasons of her frustration is that Mary believes that she is neither getting enough support from her husband, a mostly absent professor, to raise their four teenage children, nor from James, who is not approving the budget to hire more scientists (factors).

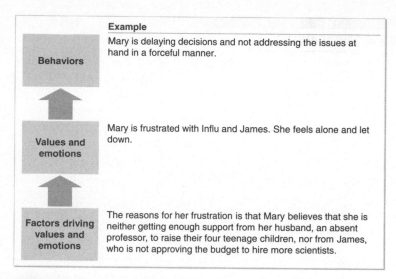

Example

Behaviors
Mary is delaying decisions and not addressing the issues at hand in a forceful manner.

Values and emotions
Mary is frustrated with Influ and James. She feels alone and let down.

Factors driving values and emotions
The reasons for her frustration is that Mary believes that she is neither getting enough support from her husband, an absent professor, to raise their four teenage children, nor from James, who is not approving the budget to hire more scientists.

FIGURE 7.1   Behaviors, Values, and Emotions, and Factors Driving Them

With this framework in mind, we can structure the deliberate act of inspirational leadership following three steps.

The first step is *connecting with the inner motivators*—values and emotions—to understand what drives them. There are different approaches to assessing values and emotions, ranging from observing physical manifestations, to words used, to patterns of behavior (which we discussed earlier in the book). In this chapter we explore empathic exploration, a simple technique that allows you to rapidly "go deep," quickly surfacing other people's inner motivators (values and emotions) as well as the factors driving them.

Second, *getting others to commit to action* by either (a) addressing the factors driving their inner motivators, or (b) by directly changing their inner motivators—values and emotions. Here we discuss the concepts of role modeling and of emotional contagion.

Third, *empowering others to act* by delegating decisions, making them accountable, and letting them solve problems, make decisions, and take risks.

UNDERSTANDING INNER MOTIVATORS— EMPHATIC EXPLORATION

The first step in inspiring others is to connect with their inner motivators—their values and emotions—and to understand the factors driving them.

Let's explore the inner motivators, looking at values first, and then discussing emotions.

Good and Evil: Values

Values and priorities reflect a person's sense of right and wrong, good and evil, important and unimportant, or what "ought" to be. "Equal rights for all," "Excellence deserves admiration," and "People should be treated with respect and dignity" are examples of values.

Some values are physiologically determined and people normally consider them objective, such as a desire to avoid physical pain or to seek pleasure. Other values are seen as subjective and they vary across individuals and cultures. People hold many other types of values: moral, ideological (religious, political), social, and more.

Although values relate to norms, they are more general and abstract. Norms provide rules for behavior in specific situations, while values identify what you judge as good or bad. While norms are the standard patterns, rules, and guidelines of expected behavior, values are intangible concepts of what is important and worthwhile. For instance, flying the national flag on a holiday is a norm, but it reflects the value of patriotism. Or, wearing dark clothing and appearing solemn are normative behaviors at a funeral, and they uphold the value of showing respect and sympathy.

People form and change their values over time. According to sociologist Morris Massey,[1] people form the "bulk" of their values during three significant periods: the imprint period (from birth to age seven), the modeling period (from age 8 to 13), and the socialization period (from 13 to 21 years). The culture you function in may further shape how your values develop.

If you are observant, you will notice that the things people say and do offer clues to the values they regard as important. For instance, a manager who praises others for executing well and completing tasks on time, and who always follows up punctually, may be signaling how highly he values "getting things done well on time."

Pleasure and Pain: Emotions

Over the past 20 years scientific advances in *neuroscience* have created a huge interest in the science of emotions. Experts have written plenty of books in the past two decades about the role and importance of emotions in regulating human behavior. People now widely recognize that emotions steer much of our daily decision-making and behavior, often in an unconscious way. This is particularly true in situations of stress and pressure, during which people typically act less rationally because emotions such as fear or anxiety are driving their behavior.

Emotions are universal and, interestingly, valid across cultures. People in San Francisco experience the same emotions as people in Tokyo or Kinshasa when confronted with danger. Experts think that emotions are a result of evolution, and therefore, they're something we share with many animals, at least with mammals. In the late nineteenth century Charles Darwin hypothesized in his book *The Expression of Emotions in Man and Animals* that emotions serve a purpose for humans and animals alike, in communication and also in aiding survival.[2]

Paul Ekman, a psychologist at the University of California Medical School in San Francisco, and a modern pioneer in the research of emotions, devoted much of his professional career to studying emotions and proving their universal character, and their validity across geographies and cultures. Like Darwin, Ekman argued that emotions serve an evolutionary purpose: to aid survival. For instance, sadness is a cry for help; it imposes one's suffering on others so they will provide assistance or rescue. Fear may make us freeze (hide) or flee, and thus protect us from danger. And anger may provide us with the strength and energy to fight someone or something that we perceive is attacking us.[3]

Science offers many frameworks for classifying emotions. Here we follow the one that Ekman developed. Studying people across all possible cultures, he identified a distinctive set of *basic emotions* that he finds all humans share: sadness, anger, fear, disgust, and a group of positive emotions that he calls "enjoyable emotions" (interestingly, these are much less well researched than the three emotions of sadness, fear, and anger, despite the recent surge of positive psychology).

While we all experience the same emotions, the experience and intensity of these emotions vary significantly between individuals and in different situations. The range of experiences of emotions can be very wide, even though there are only a handful of basic emotions. Each individual's experience of emotions can vary on a continuum from "weak" to "strong." For instance, when feeling sad, some people may feel a "little down," some disappointed, some discouraged, some depressed, some despairing, some helpless, and some miserable. Or when experiencing fear, some may feel a little worried, some concerned, some uncertain, some insecure, some anxious, some fearful, and some panicky.

Emotions are sometimes classified as "positive" and "negative," the latter being sadness, anxiety, anger, and disgust. Many believe that negative emotions lead to ineffective, dysfunctional behavior, a claim that scholars of positive psychology make frequently.

While this may be true for extreme and persistent forms of sadness (depression), anxiety (extreme shyness or paranoia), and anger (violent behavior), in normal intensities the so-called negative emotions are necessary for normal human functioning (such as allowing compassionate behavior, avoiding overly risky choices, staying away from danger, or fighting to protect oneself or others).

Moreover, negative emotions are often the somewhat surprising source of human greatness and advancement: Steve Jobs wasn't usually a happy camper, the great philosophers from the classical Greek to the modern existentialists were often troubled souls, and the French revolution wasn't brought about by optimists with positive feelings, but by angry people taking to the streets. Interestingly, insiders often describe many of the most successful individuals at McKinsey as "insecure overachievers"—those whose anxiety is the very source of the energy that impels them to extraordinary achievements.

In short, no emotions are good or bad. Each emotion serves a purpose and is essential for normal social and human functioning. Therefore, each emotion can be beneficial or it can be harmful, if it develops into an extreme or persistent state such as depression or paranoia.

Emotional mastery is an important skill for inspirational leaders. Mastery means having the ability to access the full range of emotions and their benefits without falling victim to extreme forms of any emotion.

Empathic Exploration

Understanding other people's emotions requires empathy, the affective and cognitive skill of recognizing, appreciating, and interpreting others' feelings. Empathy requires the ability to experience the world subjectively from another person's perspective. It doesn't mean understanding how it would feel to walk in the other person's shoes; instead, it's the ability to sense and connect to the other person's inner motivators and the factors driving those motivators.

To do so, you can utilize a process that uses questioning and probing to zoom in on the inner motivators someone is experiencing and to identify the context and issues driving them.

Let's illustrate this with a situation.

Hans, the consultant, is meeting Ulla, the CEO of a company he serves. She says: "Well, we had a board meeting yesterday. It was a bad meeting. They told me that my leadership succession pipeline is weak. They are driving me nuts!"

How would you react? What would you say?

Let's review some typical answers:[4]

1. *"You know how boards are; next week you'll be their hero again."*
2. *"Would you like some help with this succession problem?"* or *"I'm sorry to hear that."*
3. *"What happened exactly?"* or *"Why did they say that?"*
4. *"They're driving you nuts . . . ?"* or *"Well, that must annoy the hell out of you."*

5. "Yeah, you could always count on them, and now I guess you just don't know where you stand . . . ?" or "With all that you have done for them, now this. This must upset you!"

The answers are offered in an order of increasing empathy, with the fifth being the most empathic answer. Why? Let's review the answers.

1. The first responses offer a message that says, "Don't feel the way you do." While such messages are often delivered with good intentions, that is, to reassure or calm down the person being influenced, in essence the first response doesn't accept Ulla's emotions or show the influencer's ability to share them.
2. The second pair of responses is designed to fix the problem or to commiserate. Again, while offered with good intentions, the influencer isn't accepting or sharing the emotions of the person he's trying to influence.
3. The third set of answers come in the form of neutral questions designed to elicit more information. This typically starts with a how, why, when, or what. While a "3" answer is helpful for getting additional information on the situation's context, the influencer still doesn't share the other person's emotions.
4. The fourth set of statements is an empathic answer. The influencer acknowledges a single feeling underlying what Ulla—the person being influenced—is saying. These statements acknowledge that she is experiencing an emotion. In essence, it is as if the influencer said, "I hear you. I somehow feel what you are feeling."
5. The fifth pair of responses constitutes a very empathic answer. The influencer is sharing a wider set of feelings involved in the experience Ulla is conveying. The influencer understands her context and emotions and is acknowledging them more widely.

Empathic exploration is a process of using a series of "4s" and "5s" to zoom in on the inner motivators someone is experiencing and to explore the situation and issues driving them. The influencer may also use a "3" at times, but an empathic exploration calls for primarily using "4" and "5."

Let's illustrate the concept with two conversations: a normal one and one that builds on empathic exploration.

Normal Conversation

"We had a board meeting yesterday. It was a bad meeting. They told me that my leadership succession pipeline is weak. They are driving me nuts!" says Ulla.

"But your succession pipeline is not weak. You know that and I know that. We worked extensively on it together. I know all key executives personally. These are great executives," her consultant Hans responds (a level "1" answer).

"Thanks for saying that. I appreciate your view, you know. But I am irked about the chairman's comment that my ability to judge people is poor," says Ulla, who clearly seems irate.

"You shouldn't be irritated. Who is he to know? He didn't have a great track record in selecting people at his old organization. Believe me when I say that your judgment of people is great, at least as good as mine," Hans answers (a level "1" again).

"Well . . . thanks for your view. I appreciate your support."

"You know what I think you should do? You should review the pipeline, and gather relevant facts on the various candidates in the coming four weeks. After that you can give a revised presentation to the board. You'll have all the facts to convince them. My firm can help you with that. Also, you recall that I know the chairman and some of the board members quite well. I can also speak to them to promote your revised transition plan. What do you think?" asks Hans (a level "2" response).

"Well . . . I'm not sure. Maybe. I need to think about it. Why don't you send me a proposal?" Ulla says, withholding her trust.

Empathic Exploration   Let's try that conversation again, only this time Hans exercises empathetic exploration:

"We had a board meeting yesterday. It was a bad meeting. They told me that my leadership succession pipeline is weak. They are driving me nuts!" says Ulla.

"They are driving you nuts . . . ?" Hans acknowledges the single emotion Ulla just shared (a "4").

"Yes! You know how much work we put into it. I have really developed a great pipeline. I reviewed all candidates personally, and synced all the findings with the chairman. And now this! He didn't even warn me," sputters Ulla.

"I reckon you are irritated about this?" says Hans, again acknowledging a single feeling ("4").

"Irritated? More than that! I am angry! The chairman questioned my judgment of people in front of the entire board! That is unacceptable," says Ulla, who seems to be getting more and more angry.

"With all you have done for him. . . . You must feel betrayed!" Hans answers ("5").

"Yes, exactly! I am angry and I feel betrayed by him. He criticized me in the board meeting. I am irritated that now they have the wrong view of me. It's not the first time. He spoke negatively about me a week ago to some of my direct reports. They told me afterward and it felt very awkward. My relationship with the chairman isn't going well. It is a huge problem," responds Ulla who is now emotionally engaged and present.

"You feel this may jeopardize your effectiveness as CEO?" Hans asks ("4").

"Yes, very much so! If this becomes visible to the organization it will be hard for me to implement the strategy and turn the company around. I can't work in such a situation. It drives me nuts! I am really angry, but I have to get over it. I don't want to leave and I don't want to fight, either. I want to improve my relationship with him, and I need to. What would you advise me to do?" asks Ulla.

"I know him well. Why don't I sound him out and try to find out what is going on? After that I think you may need to have an open discussion with him," Hans responds with a "2" because Ulla asked for a solution.

"That would be great! Thank you so much, Hans. I really appreciate you listening to me and helping me on this," says Ulla.

––––––––

What do you notice when you compare the two conversations?

First, in the first sample conversation, Hans did most of the talking, denying (*your succession pipeline is not weak*), telling Ulla not to feel the emotion she is experiencing (*you shouldn't be irritated*), and providing solutions (*you should review . . .*). Ulla doesn't say much.

Second, in the second sample conversation, Ulla is more emotionally engaged. She is more present and energized by emotions, which she is now exploring with Hans' help. Importantly, she feels listened to (*I really appreciate you listening to me . . .*).

Third, and importantly, the issue that Hans wanted to help Ulla solve has evolved and changed. By acknowledging and sharing her emotions, Hans discovers that the real issue isn't succession planning; it's Ulla's relationship with the chairman. Hans has now a fuller picture of what is going on. He understands the wider context and the fact that the weak succession plan was just the issue that prompted the discussion, but it isn't the very source of Ulla's problem: her faltering relationship with the chairman.

In summary, empathic exploration is a simple and powerful approach that uses acknowledging feelings to understand inner motivators and what is behind them more fully. It calls for identifying the wider context affecting a person. Here are a few tips that may help you when you try this approach:

- *Practice, practice, practice*—When trying empathetic exploration for the first few times, you may find that it doesn't come naturally. That's because most people do not use it regularly. Like any other skill, what doesn't get practiced doesn't develop. However, while it may feel unnatural, it is risk-free. The person being listened to will appreciate the listening, even though you may not always choose the right words or, at first, you may identify an incorrect emotion.
- *Start with simple "4s"*—Level 4 empathetic exploration statements are relatively easy to engineer. Simply acknowledge a single emotion and use the same word the other person used in the conversation.

If the person doesn't verbally express any emotion, you can create a "4" by (1) asking yourself how that person might feel, and (a "2") offering that feeling as a tentative question to the other person ("Are you upset?"). If you pick the right emotion, the other person will be immediately engaged. If not, he or she will probably offer a correction ("I am not actually upset; I am worried that . . .") and help you find the right words to echo back.

- *Keep going*—Sometimes, after you use one or two level "4" responses, you may come to feel that you have gained a better understanding of the situation. That's probably true. But you may not have delved into the situation fully until the other person is completely engaged, has fully explored his or her emotions, and stops the conversation by asking for a suggestion or a recommendation (that is, asking for a "2").

- *Go beyond socially accepted stereotypes*—Many people "hold back" their real emotion and express a different one, in some cases to reflect what is socially acceptable. For instance, men are often more comfortable expressing anger though they really feel anxiety. Women are often more comfortable expressing sadness (even crying) when they are really enraged. Keeping the exploration going for a while will help you see below the surface.

GETTING OTHERS TO COMMIT TO ACTION—WORKING ON THE INNER MOTIVATORS

The second step of inspirational leadership is to get others to commit to action by either directly changing their inner motivators—values and emotions (the middle box in Figure 7.1), or by addressing the factors that drive those inner motivators (the lower box in Figure 7.1), or both at the same time.

Changing Inner Motivators: Role Modeling and Emotional Contagion

A leader can directly change others' inner motivators without necessarily addressing the factors driving them. Through role modeling he or she can affect others' values, and through emotional contagion touch their emotions.

Role Modeling   Through role modeling a leader can exemplify and transform the values of others. This happens through identification, a psychological process whereby the individual being led assimilates a property, attribute, or value of the leader. Generally, role models are those who occupy the social role to which a specific individual aspires—an example being the way fans will idolize and imitate professional athletes or entertainment artists.

The concept of role modeling stems from social learning theory, which argues that people learn social behavior primarily by observing and emulating others' behaviors.[5] For example, in one experiment, one or more individuals would look up into the sky; bystanders would then look up into the sky to see what they were seeing. At one point this experiment was aborted, as so many people were looking up that they stopped traffic.[6] Another example is Albert Bandura's Bobo Doll experiment (this impressive experiment can be watched on YouTube). In 1971, Bandura, an influential psychologist and the "father" of social learning theory, published a study showing that children who saw an adult exercise violent behavior toward a doll (the Bobo doll) were prone to copy the aggressive behavior themselves after the adult left the room.

Role modeling means inspiring others to behave in a certain way by setting an example; leading by example; behaving as you wish others to behave; "walking through" something with someone; or showing or demonstrating how to do something.

Typical phrases of a role model are:

- "Let me walk you through this. . . ."
- "When I was in a similar position, I did. . . ."

Emotional Contagion   A leader can influence others' emotions by consciously "contaminating" those emotions.

Various researchers have shown that emotions spread whenever people are near one another. In 1981, two psychologists, Howard Friedman and Ronald Riggio, found that emotions spread among people even if they do not talk to one another.[7] In 2000, Caroline Bartel and Richard Saavedra, from the Universities of New York and Michigan, respectively, found that in 70 work teams across diverse industries and companies, people in meetings ended up sharing emotions—both good and bad—within two hours.[8]

This happens through emotional contagion, a "process in which a person or group influences the emotions or behavior of another person or group through the conscious or unconscious induction of emotion states and behavioral attitudes."[9] One view developed by psychologist Elaine Hatfield is that emotional contagion happens through automatic mimicry and synchronization of one's expressions, vocalizations, postures, and movements with those of another person.[10] When people unconsciously mimic the leader's expressions of emotion, they come to feel that leader's emotions.

While emotions are shared in an automatic and unconscious way (Hatfield and colleagues describe the emotional contagion as a primitive, automatic, and unconscious process), they can also be shared in a conscious and deliberate way, as when a leader convinces and motivates others by sweeping them up in his or her enthusiasm. In such a case, the leader's positive emotions galvanize and "contaminate" the others' emotions.

A different kind of intentional emotional contagion is by giving the group a reward, or treat, in order to alleviate their negative emotions.

It is unclear whether negative or positive emotions spread more rapidly. Some researchers have hypothesized that, as negative emotions generally tend to elicit stronger and quicker behavioral responses than positive ones, unpleasant emotions may lead faster to emotional contagion than pleasant ones. Other researchers have argued that positive emotions spread more rapidly, a reminder for leaders to maintain a positive emotional state and attitude at work.[11]

What is clear, however, is that the intensity or energy level at which an emotion is displayed matters. As higher energy draws more attention to it, the same emotion (pleasant or unpleasant) expressed with high energy may lead to more contagion than if expressed with low energy.[12] Friedman and Riggio have shown that when three strangers sit facing one another in silence for a few minutes, the most emotionally expressive of the three transmits his or her emotions to the other two.[13]

Leaders using emotional contagion galvanize others with positive emotions and energy. They display enthusiasm, commitment, dedication, and passion. They tell inspirational and exciting stories, paint an exciting or otherwise energizing vision, or speak in terms of achievement, quality, or other desirable values.

Typical statements that can be used by a "contagious" leader are:

- "This is exciting!"
- "This is inspiring! We're making a difference in peoples' lives!"
- "We are together building a world-class institution. . . ."
- "We should feel proud and energized by our achievements!"

Addressing the Factors Driving Inner Motivators

A leader can also change others' inner motivators by connecting with the inner motivators of the person he or she aims at inspiring, and by addressing the factors driving those inner motivators—factors that the leader will hopefully have discovered by means of empathic exploration. This is a more empathic approach, as it builds on the specific emotions and context that the person being influenced is experiencing.

For instance going back to the case of Mary who is frustrated with Influ and James. As mentioned above, she feels alone and let down (emotion). The reasons for her frustration are that Mary believes that she is neither getting enough support from her husband, a mostly absent professor, to raise their four teenage children, nor from James, who is not approving the budget to hire more scientists (factors). If James understands the factors driving the inner motivators, he could approve the budget or offer other forms of help in hiring scientists.

Here is how a conversation that addresses the factors driving her emotions could unfold:

"Mary, you seem concerned," says James.

"Concerned? No, I am not concerned. I am frustrated!" says Mary.

"Frustrated?"

"Yes. I feel as if everybody expects something from me, and no one is helping me. My husband only cares about his latest research project, and I am dealing with everything at home myself. Two of our sons aren't doing well at school and I have to focus on that. Also, at work, you ask me to do the impossible and you don't give me the means to succeed. You are asking me to hire great scientists but I do not have any support from HR and no budget from you! I am frustrated!"

"Mary, I didn't realize. I can't help you at home, but I can at Influ. What about if I helped you to recruit some scientists, and increased the budget for R&D?"

"Would you do that?" asks Mary.

"Of course. I'll talk to HR right away," answers James.

"James, thank you so much for listening and helping me out! I really appreciate it!"

EMPOWERING OTHERS TO ACT

The third and last step of inspirational leadership is to provide space and freedom for others to act. Inspiring leaders give direction and guidance, but do not tell others what to do in detail. People, who are inspired, act on their own will. They act in line with their own values and the emotions they are experiencing.

To exercise inspirational leadership, delegate decisions to people, make them accountable, and let them solve problems, make choices, and take risks.

Typical inspirational leadership *behaviors that empower others* may include:

- Setting stretch goals
- Delegating tasks with accountability

- Providing timely, constructive feedback
- Mentoring and developing people

                              *   *   *

We have now reviewed an approach to inspiring others and helping them change. But are all people susceptible to inspiration? Not all people may react the same way to inspirational leadership though. Some are more likely to follow inspirational appeals, while some others may require harder tactics, such as requesting and legitimating. How do you adjust your leadership style to different people?

That's what we explore next.

But before that, let's go back to James.

NOTES

1. M. Massey, *The People Puzzle. Understanding Yourself and Others* (New York: Brady, 1979).
2. C. Darwin, *The Expression of Emotions in Man and Animals*, original edition (London: Penguin Classics, 2009).
3. P. Ekman, *Emotions Revealed: Recognizing Faces and Feelings to Improve Communication and Emotional Life* (New York: St. John's Press, 2007).
4. R. Kegan, "The Colors of Emotions," *Counseling Master Class Handbook*, internal training material (New York: McKinsey & Company, 2013).
5. A. Bandura, *Social Learning Theory* (Englewood Cliffs: Prentice Hall, 1977).
6. R. B. Cialdini, *Influence: The Psychology of Persuasion* (New York: Quill, 1984).
7. D. Goleman, R. Boyatzis, and A. McKee, "Primal Leadership: The Hidden Driver of Great Performance," *Harvard Business Review* (December 2001).
8. C. A. Bartel and R. Saavedra, "The Collective Construction of Work Group Moods," *Administrative Science Quarterly* 45 (2000): 197–231.
9. G. Schoenewolf, "Emotional Contagion: Behavioral Induction in Individuals and Groups," *Modern Psychoanalysis* 15 (1990): 49–61.

10. E. Hatfield, J. T. Cacioppo, and R. L. Rapson, "Emotional Contagion. Current Directions," *Psychological Science* 2 (1993): 96–99.
11. Goleman, Boyatzis, and McKee, "Primal Leadership."
12. Schoenewolf, "Emotional Contagion."
13. Goleman, Boyatzis, and McKee, "Primal Leadership."

CHAPTER 8

Influ—Finding Empathy

Later that same Sunday night, having read Marc's paper and thought about it, James walks into the kitchen when Lizzy comes down to make her cup of tea. He is intent on engaging her in a follow-up conversation and testing some of the concepts described in Marc's note.

As she puts a cup of water in the microwave to heat up, he says, "I've been thinking about what you said, Elizabeth, honey, that you don't want to go to school tomorrow."

She looks at him, surprised. "Call me Eliz . . ." she starts, and laughs, "Well you did call me Elizabeth, at last . . . thanks."

He chuckles with her, and says again, "I was worried—you sounded somewhat irritated."

"Irritated? No, I am not irritated. I am rather frustrated, Dad," she says.

"Frustrated?"

"Well, Dad, I am. I worked so hard to get ready for the stupid biology exam and I didn't pass it! I have been beating myself up over it!"

"I hear your frustration," James says, handing her the sugar canister. "Are you disappointed?"

"No, I don't feel disappointed, at least not in myself. I know I worked hard, and I don't want you and Mummy to be

(continued)

(*continued*)

disappointed. For my part, I'm concerned about retaking the exam and that's coming up soon."

"Concerned?"

"I am more than concerned. I am afraid that I might not pass the retake. Even when I work hard, I get so stressed during exams that I can hardly think, so I don't do well. Even if I know the stuff!"

"Hmmm," James echoed back to her, "You're afraid of not passing no matter how hard you work?"

"Yes, exactly!

"That's a challenge," he acknowledges. "What do you want to do? Do you have a plan?"

"I don't know. I need to feel better prepared, so I don't get stressed out during the test. I was thinking about taking some tutorials. What do you think, Dad? Should I ask for some tutoring?"

"Well, that might work well," he affirms. "What do you think?"

"Yes, it will, I think it will work. I will get a tutor. I already asked Ms. Jackson for a few names of tutors. I'll call them tomorrow . . . but, Dad, it might get sort of expensive."

"That's fine, Elizabeth, if it helps. I know you're already trying hard."

He pauses a moment, considering how he could offer a level 2 practical response in reaction to her reaching for help. As she turned to leave with her tea, he adds, "Since you tend to get stressed during exams, what do you think about also doing some mock-up exams in the next week or two? It may give you more self-confidence."

"That's a good idea, Dad. Would you help me?"

"Of course. We can start next week."

"That's cool. Thanks."

"No problem."

Elizabeth walks away, stops in the kitchen doorway and says, "Dad."

"Yes?"

"Thanks for listening."

James smiles, "No problem."

He feels better than he has in a long time.

* * *

James starts practicing empathic inquiry with his friends and family, encouraged by his first attempt with Elizabeth.

Empathic inquiry is hard for James at first. He feels quite uncomfortable "entering" into other people's feelings and probing their emotions. During this time, Marc coaches James weekly. During their sessions, James practices empathic inquiry and they discuss his progress as he applies it more and more in everyday situations. As James continues practicing, empathic inquiry becomes easier and more natural to him (it is now stored in his "automatic system" as explained in Chapter 3).

As James carries out more empathic inquiries, he also starts to understand more fully what really drives other people. He gains a much better understanding of their emotions and what underlies them. His inner portraits of the other people at Influ become clearer, fuller, more colorful, and more differentiated.

He learns that Quentin is a former competitive ski racer. He is ambitious and losing is not in his plans. At the age of 18, he narrowly missed his Olympic shot—the gateway to realizing his childhood dream of being a professional skier—and now he plans to never lose again. Right now, winning in the market with his division is not in the cards, though. This facet of his ambition is not going particularly well. Though he lives a good life—he has a loving relationship with his long-time girlfriend Chloe, a flat he's proud of in Hampstead, an affectionate but high-maintenance dog, and enough time for flying home for the

(continued)

(continued)

occasional ski weekend—he is irritated by the slow progress of the division he leads. Though he is still occasionally frustrated with James, it seems that Quentin is primarily angry with himself. He is angry he isn't winning.

He also learns more about Mary. Mary is an MD with a scientific background. She comes from a family of scientists, her mother being a professor, and her father a Noble Laureate in biology. She is open-minded, intellectually curious, imaginative, and full of good ideas. Like her parents, she is driven by the noble cause of helping people live better lives. Her enthusiasm has fallen off, some due to Influ's inability to recruit top scientists and create a lasting impact in health care. She tries to turn off her workday worries when she goes home to her four teenage boys and her professor husband, Lionel, a prominent author and literature scholar. But at home she struggles to keep up with being a wife, a mom, and a Scout leader.

Finally, he learns what drives Jorg, who is deeply frustrated that the company hasn't given him resources to go all out. Jorg came to the field of medical devices after his first wife died of cancer. His dream after he graduated from university was to build his career with a German car manufacturer, but then a few years ago, his first wife—who had been his first love and school sweetheart—died prematurely from misdiagnosed cancer. It was a huge shock. It changed his life. He left auto manufacturing and joined Influ. He didn't want to produce cars. He wanted to make life-saving products. He's committed to combatting life-threatening diseases, and frustrated that his unit isn't getting as much traction as he was hoping. Jorg occasionally still complains that he should have received resources earlier so he could improve his division's quality.

James is starting to derive real pleasure from his new and deeper understanding of others. Also, as he understands what drives the three divisional heads better, he naturally starts appealing to their inner motivators and addressing the factors driving them.

Quentin's inner motivator is anger, particularly when things aren't going well in his division. The factor driving this anger is that—Quentin being an action-oriented, ambitious, and competitive individual—he is not winning. Instead the Japanese competition, and—as he Quentin tends to personalize conflicts—one Japanese CEO and the company he leads are taking away Influ's share of the market. James decides to arouse and redirect Quentin's anger by focusing him on beating his Asian competitor.

Mary is primarily tired and frustrated. Mary struggles as a woman in a man's world, in her father's world of professional research. She struggles as a wife of a professor, who due to his research is seldom at home, and even when he's present is often absorbed in his own thoughts. She struggles as a mother of four teenage kids, two of them requiring a lot of attention as they are not doing well at school.

She also feels overwhelmed and left alone in managing the turnaround of her division at Influ. James increasingly feels comfortable naming her frustration and in tackling the factors driving it. "With all you have to do and handle, it must tiring. It must be frustrating not to get any help," he says, "but I am willing to help you as much as I can. I've identified four top scientists, genetics guys, three in the US and one in Switzerland. I have spoken to them. I think that we can succeed in hiring them if we build them a new state-of-the-art lab—and I'm willing to fund that."

Jorg is a person who values achievements and friendship. At the same time—and driven by the dramatic loss of his first wife—he has sworn to himself that he wants to dedicate his life to fighting deadly diseases. His inner motivator is that he wants to make a difference to patients. After months of practicing empathic inquiry James knows how to engage Jorg now. "Your help was instrumental before and during the turnaround.

(*continued*)

(*continued*)

It made a real difference. I've relied heavily on your friendship. Thank you for that," he says, "and I know you want to expand more broadly into life-saving devices. I've talked to Carl and that's fine with us."

James feels increasingly comfortable with his team. Quentin, Mary, and Jorg are increasingly engaged and motivated. They feel that James is listening to them, and that he is helping them to address the issues they are struggling with.

*   *   *

Yet, despite the increased engagement of James' team, the situation at Influ isn't developing as he had hoped.

Targeting Inspirational Appeals

Influ—"They want you out"

"They want you out."

"They are going to fire me."

James is sitting on the couch in his living room, seeing Friday night turn into Saturday as he thinks the same thoughts over and over, sick with worry. He is anxious about what may happen at next week's board meeting. Outside it is raining, and it is so pitch black that he can't see the London city lights from the big windows of the house. The kids are asleep and Joanne is trying to calm him down.

Given his agitation, she doesn't mention the allergy issues that are plaguing little Max. It is spring and he is having a hard time with his pollen allergy, but Joanne has always handled the kids' concerns; James never has time for all that.

She turns to her husband and says reassuringly. "They're not going to fire you—of course not. That makes no sense. You've done a great job in the past few years. If it weren't for you, Influ would never be where it is today. You know it, and they know it," she says.

"Yes, but the board told me that the Singapore debacle would have consequences. They said that I should have consulted with them before making such big investments," replies James. "And they may be right. It certainly turned out badly."

(continued)

(*continued*)

"Be that as it may, those things happen in business. And, this is your first mistake since you took over as CEO. They may reprimand you or, at worse, not pay you a bonus this year. They won't fire you for that!"

"They told me."

"Even so, it's not a tragedy. We'll find something else. You will surely get another CEO position somewhere else. Don't worry."

But James worries.

Just last week, James' world had been perfect. He was on a roll. His had managed to reengage his management team, and the company was back onto a growth path. Quentin had beaten back his Asian rivals and seemed steadier as a leader. He's relishing his extra work with Jane in strategy and even offered some good ideas. Mary had restaffed some of the critical top positions in her labs with excellent talent, though she was still looking for a few breakthrough big names. And, Jorg remained a staunch friend. His team had a run of real innovation as they rebuilt the quality of Influ's medical devices. They also completed the acquisition of a small company that makes devices that patients use to self-administer medications. And James spoke often to Marc Jansen, who had become an important touchstone.

Then the auditors raised a red flag. In Carl's office yesterday, with James present, and in an emergency board meeting later that morning they'd presented the findings of their review of Influ's Singapore operations. Due to wrongdoings by local managers, the Singapore unit had an unaccounted for deficit of millions of dollars on its books. Influ would have to restate its last-quarter results and would now—for the first time in 15 years—show a decline in quarter profits.

Carl was beyond furious. The chairman claimed, rightly, that James had pushed through the Singapore unit's management appointments and its investments without much consultation with him or with the board. James knows he made a mistake.

"We have to discuss your future at next week's board meeting. There is a trust issue. Several of my colleagues on the board feel betrayed and they're furious. They want you out," Carl barked at James just after the directors discussed the auditors' presentation.

At that moment, James felt a petrified knot in his stomach, and his mind went blank. As Joanne knew, Carl had always been James' mentor; he'd recruited James to Influ and brought him along. James understands that if he's lost Carl's respect and support, he's sunk.

After hours of conversation and sharing most of a bottle of good Cabernet along with as much reassurance as she could offer, Joanne goes up to bed. Her last suggestion is that James set up an appointment to brainstorm with Marc.

James sits on the couch staring out of the window into the bleak darkness. Carl's words echo in his head: "They want you out."

What will happen now? Influ is going to restate the last quarter's results. This has never happened before.

"They want you out."

What will his Dad say? Will he be disappointed? How will his friends react? Will they stand by him? And how will the children react when other kids mention his firing at school? Oh, the kids—he couldn't think about them now. . . .

"They want you out."

The family might have to move to another part of the country. James could be forced to sell the house after all of Joanne's hard work to make it warm and gracious. The English real estate market situation isn't really favorable, though. He could end up selling at a big loss. It would be messy. And he knows that although Joanne didn't bring up their issues with Liz, moving would be absolutely the wrong thing for a teenager who so badly needs stability and security. He couldn't even consider that while he was so preoccupied with business . . . having an uncooperative,

(continued)

(*continued*)

sulky child felt as bad as having an uncooperative, sulky board—except that he understood the board.

"They want you out."

Could he get another job as a CEO? The Singapore debacle was a mess, for sure. Could he get another job at all?

"They want you out."

Past 1 AM, past 2 AM, James still sits on the couch in the living room—alone in the dark with his thoughts spinning. Famously fearless and even good-humored in the face of negotiating teams, testy suppliers, or disgruntled executives, now he's afraid about what is going to happen. James feels weaker, as if he is losing blood and weight all at once. He is on an emotional downward spiral, imagining the worst.

Hauling himself up to bed at last, he acknowledges that Joanne is right. He needs help. Before he stretches out, he picks his cell phone up from the bedside charger, shoots off a quick text to Marc Jensen, and finally turns off the light.

* * *

The next morning, with Marc's welcoming text in hand, James—exhausted from his sleepless night—grabs a coffee and goes to see the psychologist at his office in a stately old house near the City.

Since their chance meeting on the plane, the two men have spoken often. James has learned that Marc had an impressive academic career, earning a PhD in psychology at Oxford and a doctorate in business administration at Harvard, teaching leadership at Princeton for a while and then coming home to England to teach at the London School of Economics. Now, along with his academic writing, he's running a leadership consultancy that has branched into seminars, publishing, and executive search. His firm is developing very successfully.

"Hi Marc, thank you for making time for me. I know you're busy and it's awfully short notice, but I'm in a panic and I appreciate you being available."

"No worries, James. I usually leave the very beginning of the day open so I can plan and think. Tell me, what's up?"

James explains the situation with the board as calmly as he can and confesses, "I really screwed up. I hurt the company, infuriated Carl . . . the chairman, we've talked about him . . . and now I'm afraid I'll soon be looking for a new job."

"I see. It must be stressful for you and your family."

"Yes, it is. And I see the strain on the family. I'm also worried about whether I could even find a new job at this level."

"You are worried about that?"

"Yes . . . probably I am more than worried. I am very much afraid that if I get fired from Influ, I won't find another good job."

"Hmmm. . . . I understand. We can talk about that. But let's deal with the situation at hand: what makes you think that you will get fired?"

"They told me."

"Did they, really?"

"Well, kind of. Carl told me that they would be discussing the consequences of the Singapore debacle at the next board meeting."

"I see. However, as I'm listening to you, I am a bit puzzled. That the board would fire you for the Singapore mistake seems to be at least odd. I understand it's horribly expensive, but Influ is a big corporation—the impact will pass in a quarter or two. I would expect you to get a warning, maybe a reprimand. But firing? Can we talk about the situation a bit?"

"Yes, of course."

"Let's discuss your board. Which board members want to fire you?"

(continued)

(*continued*)

"Well, I have good relationships with most of the board members. But Carl, the chairman, dominates them. He's my mentor, or he used to be, and my predecessor, the one who really created Influ in the 1990s. He is highly respected by the other members. Now, I think it's Carl who really wants me out. That's a bad reversal for me, professionally and personally. If I lose Carl, I'm sunk—and I'm hurt; we were close. But in the back of my mind I'm wondering if maybe Carl, in some odd way, welcomes the mistake I made in Singapore."

"Why do you think so?"

"Well, our relationship has grown increasingly tense over the past year or so. At last year's board meetings Carl criticized me several times, though without much reason."

"I thought you and Carl got along well."

"Yes, I thought so, too. It hasn't always been like this. Carl was a caring and supportive father figure to me in the past. In fact, he hired me. He proposed my appointment as his successor when he stepped down as CEO. Carl wanted to focus his last professional years on the chairmanship, and he thought I'd be the ideal candidate to lead Influ's operations. Carl used to protect me, but that is no longer the case. He has become egoistic, impatient, and unpleasant to work with."

"Why did he change? What's motivating him?"

"I don't know, Marc . . . I really don't know."

"Can you describe Carl to me?"

"Hmmm . . . he is 63, almost 64, married, no children. He has spent most of his career in the industry. He joined Influ when he was in his mid-forties when it was a small, insignificant player. Brian Welsh, the founder, had just died and his family hired Carl—an up-and-coming middle manager at a competing firm—to run the company.

"During his two decades as CEO, Carl increased the size of the company 30-fold. He drove a number of high profile, bold, and risky acquisitions, which led to a consolidation in our industry. During that time Influ became the undisputed industry leader, and Carl was the most respected executive in it."

"Impressive," says Marc, continuing, "Talk more about his context. He is 63. When will he retire?"

"In under two years. According to the company charter, no board member can be older than 65."

"What will he do afterward? What're his plans?"

"I don't know. He doesn't have many interests outside of work. In fact, he doesn't seem to have any. He often talks about touring the world with his wife, Lillian. But nobody believes that. His marriage isn't going well. That's in the public domain. He often comes alone when we have company events to which spouses are invited. And when his wife comes along, they never talk to each other."

"Hmmm . . . tell me more. What does he value? What's important to him?"

"He is very ambitious. He always argues for giving managers stretch targets. But he also sets the bar high for himself. He works really hard, even as a chairman, and is seldom satisfied. The few times I have seen Carl really upbeat was when he successfully negotiated acquisition deals. He is quite a tough guy. Winning in negotiations is one of the most important things to him."

"I see. What else? How would you describe his personality?"

"He's not very talkative. He discloses very little about himself, his private life, or his intentions. He never talks about what's on his mind. It is hard to understand what he wants. He doesn't have kids or even many friends or a hobby. I think he plays golf now and then so he can network with other senior executives, but I don't know if he has any friends. He's well known in the City and he's a member of a couple of prestigious clubs, but he never goes to any of them except for business. I don't think he likes crowds."

(continued)

(*continued*)

"Okay, he seems to be an introvert. And you said he seldom talks about his feelings."

"Are you kidding? I have never heard him talk about his emotions! Even Joanne couldn't get him to talk. She asked him what he remembered about the day he became chairman, a huge achievement for him, and how that felt, and she got nothing from him. And you know Joanie—she could soften a rock. She even gets along with Lillian, who's pretty remote."

"Speaking of emotions, how are Carl's relationships with other people at Influ?"

"Binary."

"What do you mean?"

"He either likes someone or hates them. When he likes people in the company, he protects them even when they commit major mistakes. Some of the people he protects have been working with him for a long time and are very respectful and loyal to him. He values that respect and loyalty a lot, almost too much. Sometimes I wonder how he selected some of these people. Some of them are really incapable, real losers, but he doesn't seem to realize it."

"And what happens to the people that he doesn't like?"

"He criticizes them for even the smallest mistake. He makes their life in the company miserable. He goes after them until they leave."

"Is that what he's doing to you? It sounds threatening."

"Yes, it is. Very much. That is, in a way, how he's treating me now and that's exactly how I feel: threatened."

"Hmmm. . . ."

"What?"

"Thinking about our conversation and your description of Carl," says Marc, pausing, "I have a hypothesis about what's going on."

"A hypothesis?"

"Yes, but it may surprise you. Hear me out. It seems to me that Carl is in a tough spot. He must be under great pressure."

"Carl under pressure? Are you kidding? I'm the one in a tough spot! I'm the one who's about to get fired! How can you say that Carl is in a tough spot?"

"James, think about this from his perspective: Carl has given almost a quarter of a century of his life to Influ, which he transformed from an insignificant shop to an undisputed leader in a gigantic industry. He is about to retire, but he doesn't seem to have anything much to look forward to: a cold marriage, no children, no grandchildren, no friends, and no hobbies. And it is probably even worse than that. Could it be that he feels you are taking his baby away from him? Influ may be the only "child" he has. Given your recent successes, everybody is talking about you now, not him. I haven't even seen his name mentioned in any recent press reports. Could it be that, in his eyes, you're in the process of taking away his lifetime achievement, his legacy, lifting it right out of his hands? And then you give it a hard kick with this Singapore business, and you've harmed his legacy, especially since you acknowledge you didn't consult him . . ."

"Jeez, Marc. I hadn't spotted that! I've been totally caught up in my own point of view."

"Like all of us, James," Marc acknowledged. "I'm just thinking that Carl's accomplishments with Influ are very immediate and important to him. You said he values achievement. It is probably not easy to see this, as he seems to be a rather introverted guy, but intellectually and emotionally he's not moving toward retirement. He's probably never spoken to you about what Influ means to him, right? As a legacy?"

"No, never."

"He also seems to be an aggressive guy."

"Aggressive?"

"Aggressive people usually have a predisposition to feeling angry. They get irritated or upset easily. They are usually

(continued)

(*continued*)

very ambitious; they tend to be risk-takers, entrepreneurs, generally people who build things. They enjoy negotiations, confrontations, and competitions. In fact, they tend to see the world as a battlefield, and to categorize others as either enemies or friends—that 'black and white' viewpoint is what you called 'binary.' They protect their friends as long as those friends remain loyal to them. They fight their enemies. The people they don't like often feel their hostility when they're together. There's nothing subtle about aggression."

"Yes, that sounds exactly like him!"

"If so, it could well be that he is angry with you, not just mad about the Singapore error, but more deeply angry. It seems that no one still associates Influ's recent successes with him; they give you the credit. Now, however, he maybe sensing that he's going to take some blame from the board for this Singapore situation. He was your mentor, and you were his chosen successor. Now you may be stealing his 'baby,' his only big lifetime achievement, and doing it harm.

"Now, he may feel that you have betrayed him and it. He is probably furious, but he isn't telling you because he doesn't talk about—or maybe even admit to himself—what he's feeling. Carl may see the Singapore mistake as his opportunity to get back at you, to get rid of you—and, here's another thought: it could also be his last chance to step forward in a crisis and be Influ's hero one more time."

James took a deep breath. "Damn! I never thought about the situation this way. I was so excited about the recognition and praise I was getting after the recent improvements at Influ that I didn't notice his increasing alienation . . . I feel so stupid! I'm really, like, apologetic about this. I never meant to harm Carl or cut him out. He did so much for me. The fact is, I owe him everything. . . ." James pauses, and after a few minutes, he asks Marc, "What do I do now?"

"Maybe we should take a break and think about all this. Why don't we meet tomorrow to discuss a possible course of action? In the meanwhile, so you can get ready, I'll give you my WAPL paper. That's a convenient acronym for What Are People Like? . . . It lays out a few questions that can help you diagnose what's going on with someone else. I developed it some time ago. It may be helpful."

"Yes, let's meet tomorrow. I need time to think . . . and I'll read it overnight. I can't believe this whole thing could be personal. . . ."

Handing James a sheaf of paper, Marc says, "Everything's personal."

CHAPTER 10

What Are People Like?

"Human beings are incredibly complex, and every individual is unique . . . however, it is possible to develop tentative perspectives quickly, that is, to reach an educated and informed hypothesis about someone else's behavioral patterns."

MARC JANSEN'S WAPL—OR "WHAT ARE PEOPLE LIKE?"—PAPER STARTED WITH A CASE HISTORY:

Nigel Jackson was born into a family of nice, modest, humble people. His father was a line manager at the local production site of a car manufacturer. His mother was a housewife. The Jacksons were very religious and valued behaviors such as caring for others, being humble, being composed, and not showing emotions or standing out from the crowd. Since Nigel's birth they had instilled these values in their only child. But Nigel was different. He was a very gifted student, the best in his class, and the top athlete in his school. He was tall, very handsome, and charming. He naturally stood out amid his peers and attracted the attention of all the girls. Nigel was a winner and a natural leader. And that's how he started to behave as he grew up. He took pleasure in displaying his superiority, winning competitions of any sort, and belittling his opponents.

(continued)

(*continued*)

He was emotional, arrogant, and domineering. He felt like a strong young lion.

Then at 16, Nigel was diagnosed with cancer. Given his youth and overall fitness, he had felt well until the cancer was pretty far along. With such a late diagnosis, for a while it seemed that Nigel would die. He and his parents went to church a lot trying to find relief and comfort in this situation. Nigel unconsciously came to believe that his cancer was a punishment for having dominated others, for having been mean and arrogant. But then, miraculously it seemed, he survived and was cured. But he was a different boy now. He became very agreeable, caring, humble, always composed, always aiming low, and never standing out. He was deeply risk-averse and avoided competitions or fights at any price. In time, no one remembered the former hearty Nigel, the athlete and leader. He was just good old Nigel who disappeared in a crowd.

Nigel went to college, married early, had children, and lived a pretty good life. He had a decent career in accounting, though he often said he wasn't entirely happy and that he was sometimes bored. Without knowing why, he was drawn to leaders and fascinated by people who took risks, fought competitors, and won. He deeply admired them, though he couldn't explain why. Once, talking to Annie, his wife, Nigel described himself as a lion in a cage. She encouraged him several times to take more risks, to be more forceful at work, and to seek more leadership roles—particularly when he had a shot at becoming the CFO of his company. While he somewhat agreed, he never did anything about it. He couldn't explain why. Nigel never stood out; it just didn't feel right to him.

Each of us has a story like Nigel's. Each of us has a set of circumstances and events that have come to shape us as individuals. Those circumstances and events are coded into our *inner operating model*, a set of beliefs and routines that influence how we behave and experience life. Each person's inner operating model is composed of a set of *underlying assumptions*, along with *mental and emotional patterns* or routines that are unique to us.

Nigel's underlying assumption was that when he sticks out, when he tries to dominate others and win, he will be punished. His mental and emotional routines became such that he felt uncomfortable leading others or taking risks. And as a consequence, he didn't. Even though he sometimes would have liked to be another person, more of a winner, he behaved "as one should": humble, modest, and agreeable. This is not rational, but he simply couldn't do otherwise.

As with Nigel, our inner operating model, the underlying assumptions and patterns of our thoughts and emotions are largely unconscious, yet—as we have seen with Nigel—they influence our daily behaviors in a powerful way. But they are not the only factors influencing our behavior.

Our behavior is affected by many more things: our context—particularly, what we are trying to achieve—and others' expectations of us. Our knowledge and experience, and our skills (what we are good at) are also important factors influencing how we behave, collaborate, interact, and work every day.[1]

In this chapter we focus on understanding why people behave the way they do. With this in mind, you can learn to read people better, to understand what they are like, and to predict how they may behave.

To begin, we will use the WAPL framework, which builds on scientifically grounded and well-proven concepts and tools. It asks a set of questions grouped around four important factors that drive human behavior: the context of the behavior, knowledge and past experience, skills and abilities, and that inner operating model or mind-set. In short, context, know-how, skills, and mind-set.

The framework is illustrated in Figure 10.1.

Consider these four factors one by one.

CONTEXT

When "reading" someone, give an appropriate weight to the person's context or situation. You can take several perspectives. Here are a few relevant (but not exhaustive) angles:

- *What might be the person's motivation? What might be at stake?*
  In any specific situation, a certain motivation drives each person, a psychological condition that arouses that individual's move

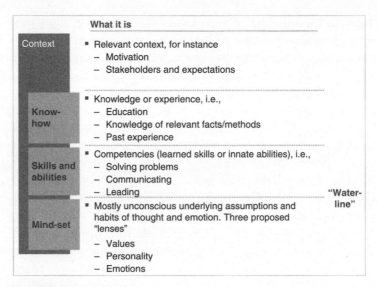

FIGURE 10.1   WAPL Framework

toward a desired goal. Motivation is the driving force of behavior and the psychological cause of personal action.[2] For example, hunger is a motivation that elicits a desire to eat. Motivation may be rooted in basic physical needs, such as eating, sleeping, or sex. Or it may be rooted in more complex, abstract needs, such as creating a piece of art or writing a book. Similarly in the business world, the "stake" that motivates your actions could be rather simple and immediate (perform a task, achieve a daily objective), or complex, overarching, and long term (secure a legacy, build a company). Any attempt to explain and predict behavior starts from a good hypothesis of what is at stake for the person you're trying to read and subsequently to influence.

- *What expectations do others have of the person?* Who are the stakeholders (superiors, peers, teams he or she leads, family) and what do they expect?
- *What is the organizational context?* How is the organization structured? Who does the person report to? Who reports to him or her? What team does he or she belong to (executive committee,

functional leadership group, working group)? What is the composition of these groups?

- *What is the culture of the organization?* This factor typically matters a lot. For instance, people working in an organization with a strong culture of following through on commitments and of being responsible are more likely to act in a conscientious way.
- *What are the group and interpersonal dynamics?* People never act in isolation; they generally behave in interaction with other individuals. If an anxious person is in a group with one or two rather confrontational and aggressive persons, he or she is likely to feel threatened and to behave in a way that might be interpreted as being introverted.
- *How do other people think this person is doing?* Is he or she seen to be performing better or worse than expected?
- *Is the person under pressure?* Under pressure, emotions can take over and people may stop acting rationally. As discussed earlier, recent advances in neuroscience show that being under pressure impedes the parts of the human brain that allow rational thinking, and it activates other parts of the brain, those that control emotion—in particular the limbic system, which includes the amygdala. Under pressure the amygdala activates strong emotions and activates the "survival response" ("fight-flight-freeze"). It triggers physiological and physical reactions (a "knot in the stomach," the "sensation of losing blood"), and causes people to think less rationally (as when you feel your "mind going blank").

KNOW-HOW

People are more likely to behave in line with what they know and with their past, positive experiences. Know-how and experiences that are relevant to leaders in a corporate context may include:

- Understanding the industry's value drivers and trends.
- Understanding the customers and the growth markets (for instance, a supply chain manager knows emerging markets).

- Having the relevant technical knowledge (such as expertise in marketing or R&D).
- Having the relevant education (some jobs require a scientific background).

Typical questions in diagnosing a person's behavioral tendencies may include:

- What did the person do in the past?
- What units and functions did he or she run?
- Was the person successful in running those units?
- Has the person already been in a similar situation to the one facing him or her today? For instance, was the person already a leader in a turnaround situation?
- Ask, what did the person do? Was it successful? How did he or she behave then?

SKILLS

People usually behave in ways that build on their skills and abilities, such as:

- Solving complex problems effectively
- Making sound decisions
- Building high-performance teams
- Communicating positively and engaging the organization
- Inspiring people to higher performance
- Ask, what is the person skilled in? What is he or she good at?

YOUR MIND-SET: UNDERSTANDING THE INNER OPERATING MODEL

As seen with Nigel in Dr. Jansen's case history at the beginning of this chapter, our mind-set or inner operating model may drive much of our behavior based on a set of underlying assumptions and habits of thought and emotion.

These underlying assumptions and habits are mostly unconscious.[3] You can't observe them directly. As with an iceberg, the majority of their heft is invisible ("below the waterline"). The Clinical Paradigm[4] of Manfred Kets de Vries, a psychologist and renowned professor at INSEAD, and the kind of deep questioning clinical psychologists use is probably the best approach to understanding your operating model. Most people aren't trained psychologists and they're seldom in a situation where they could apply deep questioning to others.

However, as with an iceberg, you can observe a part of someone's inner operating model. Since underlying assumptions and habits of thought and emotion influence language and behavior, people's speaking and behaving patterns provide clues to understanding what is going on inside their emotions, below the waterline. Many models use various constructs of language, tests, and behaviors to infer what is below the waterline, including a person's cognitive stage of development, values, personality, feelings, and so on.

Personality theories are the mainstream approach to understanding mind-sets. These theories focus on explaining behaviors that individuals exhibit consistently over time. They predict human reactions to other people, as well as stress, crises, and problems.[5]

Now, let's add two more lenses to personality theories: values and emotional dispositions. They play a pivotal role if you want to lead through inspiration and to understand the people you're leading.

PERSONALITY THEORIES

The study of personality probably started with Hippocrates' "Four Humours" theory, which postulated that a person's personality was based on the balance of four bodily humors: yellow bile, black bile, phlegm, and blood.[6] Choleric people had an excess of yellow bile, making them short-tempered. High levels of black bile were thought to cause melancholy and pessimism. Phlegmatic people were believed to have an excess of phlegm, leading to their sluggish, calm temperament. Finally, people thought to have high levels of blood were seen as sanguine and were characterized by their cheerful, passionate dispositions.[7]

Over the last 100 years psychologists have spent a lot of time and effort exploring the concept of personality, and as a result they've developed a myriad of different tools and frameworks to describe it (such as Freud's id, ego, and super-ego framework, Myers-Briggs' MBTI, and Ashton and Lee's HEXACO).

The Big Five personality framework is the one based, probably, on the most research. Known to be reliable, comprehensive, empirical, and data-driven,[8] it is the personality model most widely accepted by psychology scholars and, increasingly, by practitioners.

The Big Five personality factors are: 1. Openness, 2. Conscientiousness, 3. Extroversion, 4. Agreeableness, and 5. Neuroticism.[9] The acronyms professionals commonly use to refer to these five dimensions or factors are OCEAN, NEOAC, or CANOE. Although you can describe a person in terms of these five factors, they are not black-and-white categories. All five factors are measured on a scale, as continuous dimensions. For instance, an individual can be a strong extrovert and agreeable, but not very conscientious or open-minded. The position on each dimension is often presented as a percentile score.

Let's explore the five factors:

Openness

This is a general appreciation for art, emotion, adventure, unusual ideas, imagination, curiosity, and variety of experience. People who score high on the dimension of openness are inventive and curious. People who are open to experience tend to be intellectually curious, appreciative of art, and sensitive to beauty. Compared to closed people, they tend to be more creative and more aware of their feelings. They are more likely to hold unconventional beliefs. Another characteristic of the open cognitive style is a facility for thinking in symbols and abstractions far removed from concrete experience.

By contrast, people who score low on the dimension of openness tend to be conservative and cautious. They tend to have more conventional, traditional interests. They prefer the plain, straightforward, and obvious to the complex, ambiguous, and subtle. They may regard the arts and sciences with suspicion or view these endeavors as uninteresting. Closed people prefer familiarity to novelty. They are often resistant to change.

How does one identify open-minded people? People who score high on openness are typically quick at grasping abstract ideas. They spend time reflecting on concepts, have a vivid imagination, have lots of great ideas, and tend to use a rich vocabulary and difficult words.

Conscientiousness

This is a tendency to show self-discipline, behave dutifully, and aim for achievement against measurements or outside expectations. The trait includes a preference for planned rather than spontaneous behavior. People who score high on the dimension of conscientiousness are efficient and organized. They like order, they appreciate planning, and they follow schedules. They pay attention to details and are exact in their work. They like to get things done right, on time and as expected. They are always prepared.

Extroversion

This is characterized by positive emotions, and the tendency to seek out stimulation and the company of others. The trait is marked by pronounced engagement with the external world. People who score high on this dimension tend to be outgoing and energetic. Extroverts enjoy being with people, and are often perceived as full of energy. They are often enthusiastic, action-oriented individuals who are likely to say "Yes!" or "Let's go!" when offered opportunities for excitement. In groups they like to talk, assert themselves, and draw other people's attention.

People who score low on extroversion tend to be solitary and reserved; they are called introverts, and they have lower social engagement and activity levels than extroverts. They tend to seem quiet, low-key, deliberate, and less involved in the social world. But, don't interpret their lack of social involvement as shyness or depression. Introverts simply need less stimulation than extroverts and more time alone. They may be very active and energetic, but not in social settings.

How does one identify extroverts? Typically, they like being with other people and being socially engaged; they talk a lot, they know lots of people, and they feel comfortable being the center of attention.

Agreeableness

This is a tendency to be compassionate and cooperative rather than suspicious and antagonistic. People who score high on the dimension of agreeableness are friendly and caring individuals who value getting along with others. They are generally considerate, generous, helpful, and willing to compromise their interests to please others. Agreeable people also have an optimistic view of human nature. The key markers of agreeable people are that they show interest and empathize with others' emotions, and they take time for others; they make people feel at ease.

Neuroticism

This is the tendency to experience negative emotions, such as anger, anxiety, or depression. It is sometimes called emotional instability. People who score high on the dimension of neuroticism are sensitive and nervous. They are emotionally reactive and vulnerable to stress. They are more likely to interpret ordinary situations as threatening, and to see minor frustrations as hopeless difficulties. Their negative emotional reactions tend to persist for unusually long periods of time, which means they are often in a bad mood. These problems in emotional regulation can diminish their ability to think clearly, make decisions, and cope effectively with stress. A lack of contentment with one's life achievements can correlate to high neuroticism scores and increase a person's likelihood of falling into clinical depression.

People who score low on the dimension of neuroticism tend to be secure and confident. They are less easily upset and less emotionally reactive. They tend to be calm, emotionally stable, and free from persistent negative feelings, though that doesn't mean that low scorers experience a lot of positive feelings. They are simply more stable in their emotional balance.

How does one identify neurotic people? The main markers for people who are neurotic are that they change mood easily and often, that they are rather pessimistic and see the glass as half empty, and that they easily become irritated, anxious, or sad.

Values

We have already touched on values in Chapter 6.

People's values are in many ways aligned with their internal or underlying belief system. They provide an internal reference for what is good, beneficial, important, useful, beautiful, desirable, and constructive. Values and priorities reflect a person's sense of right and wrong, good and evil, important and unimportant, or what "ought" to be.

As discussed in Chapter 6, values have a strong influence on attitudes and behavior.[10] For example, say that a woman who values equal rights for all goes to work for an organization that treats specific groups, such as managers, much better than the rest of the employees. She may come to believe that the company is an unethical place to work. Consequently, she may not work well or may leave the company. It is likely that if the company had had a more egalitarian policy, her attitude and behaviors would have been more positive.

How can you identify someone else's values? The way a person describes a situation, how he or she defines "good and bad," and his or her habitual behaviors all provide evidence for what may matter most to him or her.

Emotional Dispositions

You would cite "emotional disposition" to describe the fact that each person has a persistent tendency to experience a certain type of emotion.[11]

Let's start with an illustration.[12]

It is Friday evening after a long, tough week. You are tired and stressed. You are waiting at the gate hoping to make the last flight home. Getting home tonight is very important. You made a commitment to your daughter, who will be performing "The Swan" at the school theater tomorrow morning. She has been preparing for six months, and she has been telling you several times a week for several months how important it is for her that you come to the performance. You have promised that you will. And now this. The plane is delayed. It has been delayed for hours. A technical issue? Bad weather? Waiting for the flight crew whose connection is late? Who knows? All you know is that you have to get home and that you have now been waiting for three hours. It is getting late. The airport is already dark and the only plane that hasn't left is yours. You have to get home tonight.

Then an agent walks up to the counter and makes the announcement you dreaded: the flight has been cancelled. You won't be able to leave tonight and so you have no way to get home in time to see your daughter's performance. You, and all other waiting passengers, groan. The collective groan is in fact audible. Now what happens?

If you watch individual passengers carefully you will notice different emotional reactions. One middle-aged man in a suit storms up to the agent and, loud enough for everyone to hear, demands to know whether she understands how important it is for him to get to his destination. He insists on seeing her supervisor, and—red-faced by now—screams that the situation is completely unacceptable.

A young mother travelling alone with a toddler walks up to the agent and asks the cause of the cancellation. She wants to be reassured that there will, in fact, be a flight tomorrow. She expresses her concern at not being home on time to the person standing next to her.

A young man in athletic attire expresses his deep frustration to the colleague sitting with him. You hear him say, "Why does this always have to happen to me? It happened the other day and now again. Why always me?"

A college student in a hoodie bobs his head to the music coming through his earphones; he barely glances up. You hear him mumbling, "Well, whatever. I'll have a good time in town."

How would you react? Or more precisely, while your reactions may be controlled and measured, how would you feel at the very moment the agent makes the announcement? Angry, like the middle-aged man in the suit? Anxious, like the young mother? Sad about missing your daughter's performance or depressed, like the young man in sports attire? Or relaxed, like the college student?

While any given flight cancellation may be worse for some passengers than others, this example illustrates the way different people have tendencies toward different emotional reactions and experiences.

The literature on emotions suggest that individuals probably differ in how easily the emotional system becomes aroused, and that some people's feelings are more easily aroused than others, both in the intensity of response and in the types of emotions they experience.[13] Some people are more likely to be annoyed by a setback, while others tend to become depressed, and still others may start to worry. This tendency to experience a certain emotion is called an emotional disposition (Richard Davidson, professor of psychology and psychiatry at Wisconsin-Madison University, calls it an "Emotional Style"[14]).

Just as emotions influence behavior, emotional dispositions influence patterns of behavior. Observing these patterns may give us a clue about another person's emotional disposition, even before we meet. The three most frequent (and most researched) emotional dispositions are believed to involve the three negative emotions of anger, fear, and sadness. What patterns of behavior do people with these three dispositions manifest?

"Angry" people tend to be ambitious, visionary, and bold. They tend to take action to address matters that bother them. For instance, they are more likely to join a protest or an uprising. Their anger at injustice motivates them to act to bring about change. They tend to be risk-takers, entrepreneurs, and builders. However, they also enjoy competition and productive confrontations. They tend to see the world as a battlefield or a competition, to categorize others in "black and white" terms as enemies or friends (and they value their friends' loyalty), and to personalize conflicts. They are not usually the most popular people, because sad or anxious people tend to feel threatened in their presence. "They seek a good argument," and find that "hostile exchanges and verbal attacks are exciting and satisfying."[15]

"Anxious" people tend to be very collaborative, good at reading others, and adept at navigating complex social situations; they're always "scanning" the environment. They can develop enormous amounts of energy, especially to address their anxieties, so they are sometimes called "insecure overachievers." Typically, they tend to be rather shy and timid; they tend to dislike confrontations (and are therefore sometimes seen as being "political" and smooth). They tend to be risk-averse and they like to share responsibilities (that is, they often appeal to authority and rules, and they tend to create processes and committees to share responsibility).

"Sad" people tend to be very agreeable, to display a high level of empathy, and to be very collaborative. However, they also often have a low level of energy, and they may be rather melancholic and pessimistic, attracting empathy and support. Some such people may even enjoy the experience of sadness: they read "tearjerkers"; they watch movies and television programs that they think will evoke a sense of sadness.[16]

In summary, the concept of emotional dispositions is a simple framework that offers clues to what someone may feel consistently, clues that you can apply even without meeting the person if you know a bit about him or her.

However, I should add a few comments before we apply the concept of emotional dispositions.[17] First, there may be other emotional dispositions than the three mentioned above. For instance, even though this disposition doesn't appear very frequently, some people may feel content most of the time (like the student) and may not fall into the main, most frequent, anger, fear, and sadness categories. Second, some people may be more "pure" and intense in their persistent tendency to feel sadness, anxiety, or anger than others. Some people may be "extremely angry" for instance, while some others may be just "mildly angry," or even share some elements from two of the basic emotions.

OVERALL CONSIDERATIONS ON THE WAPL MODEL

You can use the WAPL sheet (Table 10.1) to "read" individuals in specific situations (using the "Case" column).

A few final considerations on the WAPL framework:

- The three concepts of mind-set are not mutually exclusive and they don't constitute a complete representation of mind-set when combined (or as a McKinsey consultant would put it: the three concepts are not MECE, that is, "mutually exclusive, combined exhaustive"). In fact, they may even overlap to some extent. For

TABLE 10.1   The WAPL Sheet

Dimension	Key Questions	Case
1. Context	<ul><li>What is the person trying to achieve?</li><li>What is at stake for the person?<ul><li>Immediately?</li><li>Longer term?</li></ul></li><li>How is the company or unit he or she leads seen to be doing?</li><li>How is the person seen to be doing?</li><li>What is the expected behavior and culture of the organization?</li><li>How is the person influenced by the people surrounding him or her (e.g., superiors, colleagues, direct reports)</li><li>Does the person seem to feel that he or she is under pressure?</li><li>Other relevant factors describing the context?</li></ul>	
2. Know-how	<ul><li>What does the person know (technical knowledge)?</li><li>What is the person's relevant past experience?</li><li>Past successes and past failures?</li></ul>	
3. Skills	<ul><li>What is the person good at?</li></ul>	
4. Mind-set	<ul><li>What is the person's personality or main traits (open, conscientious, extrovert, agreeable, neurotic)?</li><li>What values might the person hold? Is the person's behavior consistent with those values?</li><li>What is the person's most pronounced emotional disposition (anxiety, anger, sadness)?</li><li>What is the person's most salient dimension?</li></ul>	

example, one of the most consistent findings in the literature is that extroversion correlates with both the experience and expression of positive emotions.[18] Neuroticism has been correlated with the experience of negative emotions.[19] Also, individuals low on Agreeableness may be prone to feel more anger.[20] The three concepts simply represent three different lenses that can be helpful in interpreting patterns of behavior with the goal of gaining a better understanding of someone's underlying and often unconscious patterns of thought and emotion.

■ The WAPL framework for understanding others is a simple, practical framework. It does not pretend to present a comprehensive view of the functioning of human beings or of human behavior. Human beings are incredibly complex, and every individual is unique. An individual's genetic makeup and the influencing life experiences are unique to that person. Therefore, reading an individual's motivations, behaviors, or beliefs accurately is impossible. However, it is possible to develop tentative perspectives quickly, that is to reach an educated and informed hypothesis about someone else's behavioral patterns—and that's the purpose of the framework.

* * *

Now that we have discussed the WAPL model, how do we tailor the influencing approach we decide to use to specific individuals and situations?

That's what we discuss next.

NOTES

1. D. Matsumoto, "Culture, Context, and Behavior," *Journal of Personality* 75, no. 6 (December 2007).

2. D. L. Schacter, D. T. Gilbert, and D. M. Wegner, *Psychology*, 2nd ed. (New York: Worth, 2010).

3. M. F. R. Kets de Vries, *The Leader on the Couch: A Clinical Approach to Changing People and Organizations* (San Francisco: Jossey-Bass, 2006); M. F. R. Kets de Vries and A. Cheak, "Psychodynamic Approach," INSEAD Faculty & Research working paper, 2014.

4. Kets de Vries, *Leader on the Couch*; Kets de Vries and Cheak, "Psychodynamic Approach."

5. J. F. Winnie and J. W. Gittinger, "An Introduction to the Personality Assessment System," *Journal of Clinical Psychology, Monograph Supplement* (1973): 38–68; C. J. Krauskopf and D. R. Saunders, *Personality*

and Ability: The Personality Assessment System (Lanham, MD: University Press of America, 1994).

6. N. Carlson et al. *Psychology: The Science of Behaviour* (Toronto: Pearson, 2010).

7. Ibid.

8. J. M. Digman, "Personality Structure: Emergence of the Five-Factor Model," *Annual Review of Psychology* 41, no. 1 (1990): 417–440.

9. R. R. McCrae and O. P. John, "An Introduction to the Five-Factor Model and Its Applications," *Journal of Personality* 60, no. 2 (1992): 175–215.

10. M. Rokeach, *The Nature of Human Values* (New York: Free Press, 1973).

11. R. Kegan, "The Colors of Emotions," *Counseling Master Class Handbook*, internal training material (New York: McKinsey & Company, 2013); R. J. Davidson, *The Emotional Life of Your Brain: How Its Unique Patterns Affect the Way You Think, Feel, and Live and How You Can Change Them* (New York: Hudson Street Press, 2012).

12. Adapted from Davidson, *Emotional Life of Your Brain.*

13. D. Matsumoto, "Culture, Context, and Behavior," *Journal of Personality* 75, no. 6 (December 2007).

14. Davidson, *Emotional Life of Your Brain.*

15. P. Ekman, *Emotions Revealed: Recognizing Faces and Feelings to Improve Communication and Emotional Life* (New York: St. John's Press, 2007).

16. Ibid.

17. C. Feser and P. Gurdjian, "Growing Leaders. A Light-Hearted Introduction to Leadership Development," McKinsey internal publication, 2014.

18. U. Schimmack, P. Radhakrishnan, S. Oishi, and V. Dzokoto, "Culture, Personality and Subjective Personality, and Subjective Well-Being: Integrating Process Models of Life Satisfaction," *Journal of Personality and Social Psychology* 82 (2002): 582–593; P. T. Costa and R. R. McCrae, "Influence of Extroversion and Neuroticism on Subjective Well-Being: Happy and Unhappy People," *Journal of Personality and Social Psychology* 38 (1980): 668–678; R. A. Emmons and E. Diener, "Personality Correlates of Subjective Wellbeing," *Personality and Social Psychology Bulletin* 11 (1985): 89–97; R. A. Emmons and E. Diener, "An Interactional Approach to the Study of Personality and Emotion," *Journal of Personality* 54 (1986): 371–384; W. Pavot, E. Diener, and F. Fujita, "Extroversion and Happiness," *Personality & Individual Differences* 11 (1990): 1299–1306; W. Ruch, "Extroversion, Alcohol, and Enjoyment," *Personality & Individual Differences* 16 (1993): 89–102.

19. Schimmack et al., "Culture, Personality, and Subjective Well-Being."
20. M. A. Chesney, P. Ekman, W. V. Friesen, G. W. Black, and M. Hecker, "Type A Behavior Pattern: Facial Behavior and Speech Components," *Psychosomatic Medicine* 52 (1990): 307–319; D. Keltner, T. Moffitt, and M. Stouthamer-Loeber, "Facial Expressions of Emotion and Psychopathology in Adolescent Boys," *Journal of Abnormal Psychology* 104 (1995): 644–652.

CHAPTER 11

Tailoring Influencing Approaches

"People with a strong values-based orientation are ideal candidates for inspirational appeals."

Steve's head dropped and he stared at his feet. After a weighty, uncomfortable pause, he issued a challenge that would haunt me for days. "Do you want to spend the rest of your life selling sugared water, or do you want a chance to change the world?" Sculley felt as if he had been punched in the stomach. There was no response possible other than to acquiesce. "He had a uncanny ability to always get what he wanted, to size up a person and know exactly what to say to reach a person," Sculley recalled.

—From *Steve Jobs*, by Walter Isaacson

Steve Jobs was very skilled at influencing, and he knew exactly how to adjust his leadership approach to specific individuals.

In this chapter we start to develop this very skill. We discuss how to adjust your influencing approaches to specific individuals using the WAPL framework. We look at appropriate influencing approaches that work with the four elements of the WAPL framework: context, knowledge, skills, and mind-set.

CONTEXT

As discussed in Part One, the *hard tactics* of pressure, coalition, and legitimating function most effectively with individuals who are in simple, clear, static situations (required tasks are routines or standard procedures), and who feel a sense of urgency (and thus may be more accepting and understanding about the use of hard tactics).

Soft tactics work best for individuals in a dynamic, ambiguous, and complex situation. That's also when it is hard for a leader to state simple requests. In this setting, engage the individuals being influenced in developing the right course of action.

Of the soft influence tactics, *inspirational appeals* may be most appropriate in situations of pressure and stress, that is, when the amygdala is active and people are behaving "less rationally."

KNOWLEDGE

Socializing may be a powerful approach to influencing others who have the knowledge or experience required to accomplish the required task. Socializing entails telling someone that he or she has special skills or qualifications and praising past performance. Because conscientious workers tend to be competent, orderly, dutiful, self-disciplined, and achievement-oriented, they are likely to perform well.[1] And because conscientious people are more likely to have developed their knowledge and skills, and achieved higher performance, leaders are more likely to cite their performance in seeking more of the same behavior and performance.

SKILLS

For the very same reasons, *socializing* may be also powerful in influencing others if they possess the skills or abilities required to accomplish the required task.

MIND-SET

Soft approaches require tailoring the leadership approach to what is dear and important to an individual or the organization's members: personality, values, and emotional disposition.

Personality Traits

The ideal influencing approach varies by personality trait.[2]

- *Openness*—Open people are likely to be good targets for *rational persuasion*. Open-minded people are receptive to others' ideas and values. This openness offers other people easy access in order to attempt to influence or persuade them. Because open targets are likely to listen to ideas without resistance, leaders influencing them can afford to be straightforward. Rational persuasion is the most straightforward approach. Assuming the leader's logic is reasonable and comprehendible, others are likely to give the leader's arguments due consideration.
- *Conscientiousness*—Conscientious people are likely to be good targets for *socializing* tactics. As discussed before with knowledge and skills, socializing includes praising past performance. Leaders can cite past performance in seeking more of the same behavior and performance.
- *Extroversion*—Extroverts are likely to be good targets for *inspirational appeals*, because they encompass warmth, gregariousness, assertiveness, activity, excitement-seeking, and positivity.[3] Because extroverts are active and energetic, they need to be steered rather than motivated. Inspirational appeals highlight the meaningful or exciting possibilities that will accompany a given course of action, inviting extroverts to focus their energy in that direction.
- *Agreeableness*—Agreeable people are likely to be good targets for *legitimating* influence approaches. The facets of agreeableness include trust, straightforwardness, altruism, compliance, and modesty.[4] Compliance is probably the most salient trait of agreeableness. When influencing agreeable people, leaders may take advantage of this tendency toward compliance with legitimating tactics, which reinforce standing policy or prior agreements.
- *Neuroticism*—Neurotic people are likely to be good targets for *requesting* approaches. They tend to be emotionally unstable, that is, vulnerable to stress and characterized by frequent mood changes. Because those scoring high on neuroticism are unstable, it is difficult to calculate how they will respond to any given tactic. Exerting influence is sometimes metaphorically described as using

"carrots and sticks." Carrots are motivators for something positive and desired, whereas sticks are demotivators for something painful or undesired. People vary a great deal in what they desire, but they are relatively consistent in the things that they want to avoid. Requesting tactics tap into the negative motivators characterized by sticks. Requesting tactics consist of behaviors such as making demands, using threats or warnings, or nagging and constantly checking up on people. Because people who score high on neuroticism are unstable and inconsistent, leaders are likely to be more effective if they use tactics with the most consistent motivational effect, that is, requesting tactics.

Values

People with a strong values-based orientation are ideal candidates for inspirational appeals. Appealing directly to the values that matter most to them is likely to create strong commitment and devotion to an action, even if it requires effort and persistence.

Emotional Disposition

Leveraging other people's emotional dispositions means arousing their emotions; that is, using *inspirational appeals*. The leader can amplify or moderate the audience's emotions to achieve the desired commitment.

- *Anxiety*—People who tend to be anxious when confronted with setbacks are likely to be good targets for inspirational appeals that decrease or increase anxiety. This includes such statements as, "You shouldn't worry because. . . ." or "If you don't take action, there will be negative consequences. . . ."
- *Anger*—People who tend to experience anger when confronted with setbacks are likely to be good targets for inspirational appeals that decrease ("I am on your side. . . .") or evoke anger ("He is attacking you. You have to react. . . .").
- *Sadness*—People who tend to experience sadness when confronted with setbacks are likely to be good targets for offers of

TABLE 11.1 Tailoring Influencing Approach Using WAPL Framework

Dimension of WAPL Framework	Proposed Influencing Approach
Context	
Complex, ambiguous, rapid change; situations that are emotionally loaded	Soft tactics, inspirational appeals
Simple, clear, high sense of urgency	Hard tactics or simple soft tactics
Know-how, experience	Socializing or inspirational appeals
Skills, abilities	Socializing or inspirational appeals
Mind-set	
Personality trait—extroversion	Inspirational appeals
Personality trait—conscientiousness	Socializing
Personality trait—agreeableness	Legitimating
Personality trait—openness	Rational persuasion
Personality trait—neuroticism	Requesting
Values	Inspirational appeals, appealing to values
Emotional disposition—anxiety	Inspirational appeals, evoking anxiety
Emotional disposition—anger	Inspirational appeals, evoking anger
Emotional disposition—sadness	Inspirational appeals, offering emotional support

emotional support. Offering such support along with compassion is likely to be a viable influencing approach.

Table 11.1 summarizes the most effective influencing approaches, given a WAPL profile.

COMBINATIONS AND SALIENCE

An individual may have more than one trait or particular skill set. Someone may be very experienced, skilled, principled, extroverted, and anxious. Relating to someone with each of these dimensions of the WAPL framework would require a different approach. Which approach should you take?

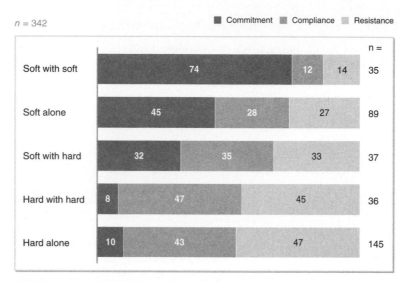

FIGURE 11.1 Outcomes of Combinations of Influencing Tactics
Source: C. M. Falbe and G. Yukl, "Consequences for Managers of Using Single Influence Tactics and Combinations of Tactics," *Academy of Management Journal* 35, no. 3 (1992): 638–652.

Leadership is seldom a one-time, one-dimensional influencing event. In fact, it often spans longer periods of time and includes several influencing attempts. And, you can easily combine influencing approaches.

In the study mentioned in Chapter 3, Falbe and Yukl also analyzed which combinations of approaches work best together. The results are summarized in Figure 11.1.

Hard attempts alone, or in combination with other hard approaches, are roughly equally effective (or ineffective) in creating commitment. Contrary to hard tactical combinations, soft combinations are very effective in creating strong commitment.

In comparison to using single soft tactical attempts, *combining soft approaches further increases the commitment level* of those who are asked to carry out specific requests.

But which influence approach should be prevalent when you use a combination of tactics?

The key question here concerns the person you want to influence: *What is that individual's most salient dimension?* For instance, is the person strongly driven by specific values? Or is the person an extreme extrovert? Or is the person frequently angry and irritable?

Salience defines the nature and tone of the overall influence strategy.

* * *

James is in trouble and needs help. After studying the WAPL framework and Marc's information about how to tailor an influencing approach to a specific individual, can James salvage his career and his relationship with his mentor? It's time for him to check back in with Marc and formulate a strategy for regaining Carl's trust.

NOTES

1. G. M. Hurtz and J. J. Donovan, "Personality and Job Performance: The Big Five Revisited," *Journal of Applied Psychology* 85, no. 6 (2000): 869–879.
2. K. M. Mullaney, "Leadership Influence Tactics in Project Teams: A Multilevel Social Relations Analysis" (PhD dissertation, Graduate College of the University of Illinois at Urbana-Champaign, 2013).
3. P. T. Costa and R. R. McCrae, "Domains and Facets: Hierarchical Personality Assessment Using the Revised NEO Personality Inventory," *Journal of Personality Assessment* 64, no. 1 (1995): 21–50.
4. Ibid.

CHAPTER 12

Influ—Winning Carl Back

James returns to Marc's office at lunchtime on Monday. He puts two Pret a Manger paté sandwiches on the table and reports, "Marc, I used your WAPL sheet to profile Carl. It was very helpful." He hands the document to Marc, with the particulars about Carl filled in:

Lens	Key Questions	Case
1. Context	■ What is the person trying to achieve? ■ What is at stake for the person? 　■ Immediately? 　■ Longer term? ■ How is the company or unit he or she leads seen to be doing? ■ How is the person seen to be doing? ■ What is the expected behavior, culture of the organization? ■ How is the person influenced by the people surrounding him or her (e.g., superiors, colleagues, direct reports)?	Carl is focused on Influ's success. ■ *He is retiring in two years.* ■ *He has little to look forward to.* ■ *Carl's legacy of having built Influ may be at stake.* ■ *He may perceive that I am stealing his only "child"— Influ—from under his feet.* ■ *He may feel I am not treating him with sufficient gratitude, deference, and respect.* ■ *He feels under pressure to assure Influ's growth.*

(continued)

(*continued*)

Lens	Key Questions	Case
	■ Does the person seem to feel that he or she is under pressure? ■ Other relevant factors describing the context?	
2. Know-How	■ What does the person know (technical knowledge)? ■ What is the person's relevant past experience? ■ Past successes and past failures?	■ *Carl is the former, successful, and iconic CEO of Influ.* ■ *He's never failed in business, at least, not so far.*
3. Skills	What is the person good at?	■ *Carl is very credible and has the ability to influence the board.*
4. Mind-Set	■ What is the person's personality or main traits (open, conscientious, extrovert, agreeable, neurotic)? ■ What values might the person hold? What is the language that the person uses to describe expectations for own and others' behaviors? Is the person's behavior consistent with those values? ■ What is the person's most pronounced emotional disposition or what mix of dispositions might the person have (anxiety, anger, sadness)? ■ What is the person's most salient dimension?	■ *Carl is rather an introvert.* ■ *He values achievements, respect, and loyalty.* ■ *He is a sort of "angry," a rather aggressive person.* ■ *Aggressiveness is probably Carl's most salient mind-set dimension.*

"I think that I understand Carl much better now" James continues, "I understand that his legacy may be at stake for him. I also understand the context of our interaction and why he may be under pressure. He is retiring in two years, he has little to look forward to, and I am stealing his only 'child'—Influ—without having outlined any continuing role for him. It also may be that I'm not being deferential, grateful, or respectful enough. And I think I understand his mind-set. Using your three lenses: he values achievements, respect, and loyalty, which is where I'm falling down. He is an introvert, and he is a rather angry guy. In fact being angry is probably his most salient feature."

"Well, if your hypothesis is correct . . ." Marc starts to say.

"Yes, of course. It may not be 100 percent correct, but I think it is accurate enough. So what is the course of action? Should I go to him and discuss his feelings toward me? Should we talk about why he's angry?"

"That's unlikely to work. Carl is an introvert and is probably feeling defensive. He is unlikely to want to talk to you about his feelings."

"What shall I do, then?"

"Well," Marc suggests, "let's use the WAPL framework. The framework postulates that four factors drive behavior: one's context, one's knowledge and experience, one's skills and abilities, and one's mind-set. Can you influence any of those?"

"Hmmm . . . let me think. I can't really change much of the context. I could, though, give him back his legacy, and some continuing role, and that would reduce pressure on him and maybe on me. I could take a less visible public role in representing Influ's achievements and results, emphasize his role more to others, and let him 'shine' more. Maybe I could even ask him to become an advisor to me once he retires. I actually do value his advice a lot."

"Yes, I agree. But that is Act II of the plan."

"What do you mean?"

"I mean that you will not be able to carry out very much of this plan before next week's board meeting. Changing others' perception of Carl's role and yours will take time. You also need

(continued)

(*continued*)

to take some action to influence his behavior before the board meeting and during it. Your plan needs an Act I."

"Yes, you're right. I can't change his knowledge and experience. I can't change his skills. And, I probably can't change his mind-set. I am stuck!"

"Are you? You may not be able to change his mind-set, but you may want to engage with him and influence him, building on your understanding of his mental habits," Marc suggests.

"What do you mean?"

"We hypothesized that Carl values achievements, respect, and loyalty. We also hypothesized that he is rather angry. In fact, you described this as his most salient feature. He probably feels you haven't been respectful and loyal to him, and he may see you as someone who has betrayed him.

"You may have to go to him, and arouse his emotions. You may have to moderate and reduce his anger by apologizing for what you have done (in his eyes). You may even have to declare your respect, loyalty, and support to him. I can't tell you how. You know him best. You have to find the right moment and the right words. This is Act I of the plan. If the board meeting goes well, you will implement Act II."

"I understand. . . . Let me think about it," James says. "In any case, I'll try to meet with him before next week's board meeting and I'll let you know how that goes. Thanks, Marc, you've really expanded my thinking and I hope we have a bit of a handle on this situation now."

* * *

A few days later Marc receives an e-mail.
To: Marc Jensen
From: James Robinson
Personal and confidential
Hi Marc,
I found an excuse to go see Carl at his home yesterday. I did what you recommended. I told him that I truly respect him, that

I look up to him, and that I want us to go back to working well together. I also apologized for not having consulted with him on the Singapore issue, and on a few other matters.

He didn't react. In fact, he was quite distant and aloof. Anyway, I left his house even more anxious than before, wondering if the whole visit was another mistake. Then today he came to see me in my office. He said he forgives me, and he's looking forward to continuing to work together with me. Imagine! He said that I shouldn't worry about the upcoming board meeting because he's going to protect me. This is fantastic!
Many thanks,
James
P.S. You're right. It's all personal.

* * *

To: James Robinson
From: Marc Jansen
Re: Personal and confidential
I am glad it worked, James. But let's wait to see what happens at the board meeting next week.

Words are important, but behavior is crucial. I am confident that it will work, though. And if it does, I suggest that you start immediately with Act II of our plan!
Regards, Marc

* * *

One week later Marc receives another e-mail from James.
To: Marc Jensen
From: James Robinson
Re: Personal and confidential
Hi Marc,
The board met yesterday and discussed the Singapore issue at length. I was sweating bullets and it was, apparently, a very emotional discussion, but Carl stood up for me. He argued that

(continued)

(*continued*)

such mistakes happen, but that the board should look at it in the context of the overall expansion strategy, which is quite successful.

He also said something that no one except him could ever have said: that the board is also partly to blame because it should have been more proactive and more involved in such an important project. In the end, the members agreed with him.

They decided to hold more frequent board reviews of crucial projects, but Carl protected me, just as he promised.

I am so relieved!

As you suggested, I am now starting with Act II of our plan.

I would like to thank you wholeheartedly, Marc. You saved my career! You just about saved my life!

Warm regards,

James

* * *

James is back on a roll. He has turned Influ around, ignited some growth spurts, and repaired his relationship with the chairman.

Unfortunately, things aren't as great as he thinks.

Inspiring at Scale

CHAPTER 13

Influ—"We have an offer"

"We have received an offer for the company. We are discussing it in the board."

After six months of stronger collaboration, increased engagement with James' top team, and moderate shots of growth, Influ seems to have slowed again.

Recently released market data for the three business units seems to suggest that Influ is going sideways again, with lots of activity, but little growth overall and importantly with no growth in market share.

Despite its investments, US players continue to out-compete Influ in molecular diagnostics and Asians are again beating it in blood diagnostics. The only business showing improvement and some growth is the Medical Devices business unit. Jorg has largely fixed the quality problems. As James expected, Jorg is so well-organized, effective, and detail-oriented that he got things done the right way, on time, and as expected.

The other two units are facing tough setbacks: Quentin's expensive new product launch failed and Mary is having a much harder time than either she or James expected in turning around the Molecular Diagnostics unit.

(continued)

(*continued*)

Somehow, it seems that even though James has managed to engage his three unit heads personally, change—maybe with some exceptions in the Devices unit—is not happening to the extent the team had hoped. There are islands of change across the organization. But it is spotty. The change process across the organization lacks consistency and momentum.

Despite Carl's support for James, the board is frustrated with the lack of progress. It is now weighing the opportunity to sell Influ to a smaller, but faster-growing competitor. Carl told James about it privately, and the phrase he used is echoing in James' head: "We have received an offer for the company. I am against selling but the board wants to discuss it."

"Discuss it? What if they sell it? What will I do? Will people think I have failed?" James worries. He needs help and by now he knows where to go.

He calls Marc and asks if they can move their usual monthly meeting to the next morning, even though it'll be Saturday. Marc is more than willing when he hears the tension in James' voice.

✳   ✳   ✳

"Thanks for fitting me in on the weekend, Marc. It's crisis time again at Influ," James says as he enters Marc's office.

"Never a dull minute," Marc nods. "Tell me what's going on."

"Well, while I feel that my team is engaged and motivated, it seems that we can't get the organization to move," James says, "what's bad is that even though Carl is supporting me, and cordially, at that, he's full of bad news from the board. I think I am losing their confidence—the company is churning money, not growing, and growth is all they want."

James doesn't mention the possible sale of Influ—because it's a listed company—but he's become comfortable over time making his personal frustrations and fear of failure clear to Marc.

"I understand," Marc says. "Have you tried to take a more inspiration-based approach with your unit heads? They're so pivotal to you and to your company—I see your need to fire them up again."

"Blast it, Marc. You know, while I have exercised empathic inquiry and started to connect with my colleagues at a more personal level, I am not sure this is enough. I feel that—while they are more engaged—the organization is not moving. Change is spotty. It is happening in some parts of the organization, but not in other parts. Change overall seems stalling."

"Got it. You sound very frustrated."

"I am. . . . What would you suggest? I think I am getting better and better at engaging and inspiring my team," James says, shaking his head. "But how can I or my team scale up our efforts to motivate the entire organization? We are running out of time. How can we get the entire organization to change faster? It's like turning the Queen Mary. We have to get Influ—the whole damn ship—to work harder toward growth! And it needs to happen fast. It's impossible!"

Marc hands James a typed paper. "Here is a short report I've written. I think you'll find it useful. It covers deploying inspirational leadership at scale. Let's meet mid-week and talk about it."

"Does it address how to accelerate change in large organizations? In Queen Mary–type of situations?" asks James.

"Yes, it does. You'll enjoy reading it."

"Thanks, Marc. I always feel encouraged when you give me homework," James finally smiles.

"You are welcome," Marc smiles in return, "and give my regards to your family."

CHAPTER 14

Inspiring at Scale

The Influence Model

> "Knowing the emotional state of an organization allows the leader to mobilize larger groups of people by arousing that state."

The greatest leader is not necessarily the one who does the greatest things. He is the one that gets the people to do the greatest things.

—Ronald Reagan

In Chapter 11 we discussed an approach to inspire others consciously and deliberately. Can it be applied to organizations? Do organizations have inner motivators? Do organizations have values and emotions?

Yes, sort of.

Each organization typically has a culture, or a set of beliefs and values, which are shared among the organization's members. Members of a company may share values such as helping others (e.g., patients, customers), integrity, respect, working effectively, and the like. Leaders can leverage shared values to mobilize people. For instance, a leader may appeal to the value of curing patients to mobilize a health industry organization to improve its performance.

Also, groups of people can share emotions. Through the process of emotional contagion described before, groups of people, organizational units, and sometimes entire organizations, develop an emotional state that becomes prevalent among all the people throughout the organization. Knowing the emotional state of an organization allows the leader to mobilize larger groups of people by arousing that state. For example, a political leader may address a nation's sense of anger and frustration to mobilize voters who seek change.

We can structure the deliberate act of inspirational leadership at scale by following two steps.

First, understanding the inner motivators of organizations—their values and emotional states.

Second, getting the organization to change by using four levers that drive behaviors of organizational members: communication, organizational structure, incentives, and capabilities. These four levers are captured in the Influence Model, a simple, yet academically well-grounded framework a leader can use to plan the steps that are necessary for their corporate transformations to succeed.

Let's explore the two steps in more detail.

UNDERSTANDING INNER MOTIVATORS OF ORGANIZATIONS—VALUES AND EMOTIONAL STATES OF ORGANIZATIONS

Let's briefly turn to the concepts of values and emotional state of organizations, and to how to identify them.

Organizational Values

In the context of organizational values, researchers and managers often refer to the concept of corporate culture. Culture as a concept is largely a matter of sociology and anthropology. They define culture as a set of values shared by groups of people or entire organizations.

You can turn to several questionnaire-based tools to measure your company's values. Also, mission and vision statements of organizations are often a good source for finding relevant values.

Emotional State of Organizations

Groups of people, and sometimes entire organizations, can develop an emotional state. As described in Chapter 7, emotions spread whenever people are near one another. If an emotion is sufficiently intense, and there is enough time for it, an emotion can spread across an entire organization, creating a shared emotion. We call this shared emotion the emotional state of the organization.

You can identify the emotional state of a group or organization by aggregating self-reports from members of the group, as well as by viewing the group from the outside and looking for emotional gestures and clues or behavioral patterns.[1]

GETTING ORGANIZATIONS TO CHANGE— THE INFLUENCE MODEL

Inspiring an organization to change is more complex than inspiring a single individual. It requires actions along a number of dimensions, communication, role modeling through leaders, investment into capabilities, and changes to the structure and incentive systems of the organization. These dimensions are captured in the Influence Model.[2] It is based on the assumptions that individuals change their behaviors when:

- One, they hear or are told, and *understand and are convinced of the reasons* for change.
- Two, they see leaders and others act as *role models* for the required actions. Role-modeling is most effective when people aspire to become like the role models, when they can relate to the role models (due to similar background, age, etc.), and when role models succeed after overcoming difficulties, rather than when they achieve success easily. Role models who succeed in seemingly difficult, challenging situations are inspiring, produce "followership," and draw followers to copy their behavior.[3]
- Three, they act using the changed behavior and while doing so, *develop the skills and abilities* to carry out the new behavior through enactive mastery. Enactive mastery, or functional or leadership competence, is defined as accomplishing repeated performance (achieving goals and learning by doing). Building the skills and abilities needed to perform a given activity

through gradual accomplishment facilitates mastery. To build mastery, leaders can set goals that their followers perceive as ambitious but achievable. Accomplishing such goals builds confidence, and gradually gets people to set more ambitious goals for themselves. Also, leaders can accelerate the pace at which people build competencies by making sure they get on-the-job coaching and mentoring.[4]

- Four, change happens through *reinforcing mechanisms*, such as having the leader set the context (remember the context dimension of the WAPL framework) for behavior. This may include changing expectations, making people accountable, improving incentive systems, and changing the organization's structure and processes.

The four dimensions of the Influence Model are shown in Figure 14.1.

A transformation that is inspiration-driven addresses the inner motivators of an organization. We can describe it using the influence model. An inspiration-driven transformation is one in which:

- First, a *change story* appeals to the values of the dominant organizational culture, or arouses emotions prevalent in the entire

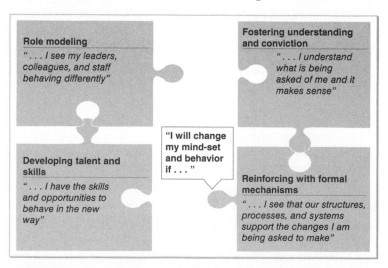

FIGURE 14.1 The Influence Model
Source: McKinsey proprietary research.

organization (emotional state). The overall change story appeals to the values that most people in the organization hold, and it touches on the emotional state of the organization.

A change story is likely to be more powerful when brought alive with emotional examples and metaphors. Leaders often compose vision or strategy statements using a list of generic phrases and facts. However, our brain has difficulty memorizing lists of blank statements or facts. It handles emotional stories and metaphors much better. "Narrative imaging—stories—is the fundamental instrument of our thought," writes neuroscientist Robert Turner. Most of our thinking, our experience, and our knowledge are organized as stories.[5] Hollywood and Bollywood tell us stories. The Bible is a story. And it is no coincidence that some of the most inspiring leaders in history have been great storytellers, such as John F. Kennedy or Winston Churchill who used metaphors and positive visions.[6]

To be powerful, a change story should be *cascaded throughout the organization* and adjusted and refined to reflect the fact that values and emotions may differ by business units, geographies, or functions. In an inspiration-driven transformation, the values and emotions of each specific unit of performance matter.

- Second, leaders throughout the organizations should be role models of the values reflected in the change story. *Each leader* of a unit, business unit, geography, or function, *role-models* the values and arouses the emotions embedded in his or her particular change story—the result of a cascading process that started with the change story of the company leader.
- Third, *building of skills and abilities* that stem from implementing the strategies embedded in the change stories empowers people. As change stories adjust to fit each unit, so do leadership and capability-building interventions.

In inspiration-driven transformations, *building competencies in people is a leadership responsibility*. As mentioned above, leaders build their people's competencies—whether functional or leadership competencies—through a process of gradual accomplishment. Leaders can help their people build competencies faster by mentoring and coaching them.

Field-and-forum capability-building programs can complement the leaders' efforts. In such programs, people attend workshops to learn new skills (forums) and apply them in their day-to-day work sometimes supported by professional coaches (field).

- Fourth, leaders structure the organizations to make people accountable and empower them to make decisions, organize their work, take risks, and innovate.

Many leaders of today's large, complex organizations have a hard time making decisions. To manage their business in different countries spread throughout various geographic regions, several large firms have introduced regional and subregional management structures. To ensure the implementation of global policies and to capture economies of scale globally, many firms have strengthened their functional "secondary" axes, such as information technology, procurement, human resources, and finance. Many also have introduced central marketing, customer-segmentation, and sales-channel functions to foster the exchange of best practices among countries and regions. Organizational models originally based on simple vertical structures—a relic of "Taylorism"—have become more complex as companies have added matrix overlays to accommodate (sometimes several) "secondary management axes." Corporations also have added ad hoc constructs such as study groups, innovation committees, or cross-unit product boards. Many large firms have developed very dense, deep organizational structures with extensive interdependencies. Often, in such circumstances, accountabilities become blurred and an enormous amount of time is wasted on internal coordination.

Leaders can simplify their organizations and empower their members several ways.[7] One is to organize based on the concept of *self-managed performance cells*. Such units have a clear performance agenda. One of the first applications of this concept was the reorganization of General Motors (GM) by Alfred Sloan, its long-standing president and chairman. In the 1950s he reorganized GM into five divisions, effectively creating five independent car companies each with its own brand and its own profit and loss statement. This allowed GM to grow and to become the world's largest corporation—at the time.[8] But the concept of performance cells doesn't stop at the divisional level. It can be, and has been, applied to business units, geographies, teams, or centralized support services (such as Procter & Gamble's "Global Business Services" or Nestlé's centralized manufacturing organization).

Performance cells at any level share three characteristics: they are guided by performance metrics, they have the autonomy to organize themselves, and they have period-based learning cycles:

1. *Performance metrics*—Depending on the specific objectives and activities of the cells, performance metrics may vary. A business unit would have a scorecard including a profit and loss statement. For lean sales or customer-management teams, the metrics might include cross-selling rates, revenue, or service quality. In lean manufacturing teams, scorecards might include default rates, scrap rates, or unit costs.

2. *Autonomy to organize themselves*—Performance cells can improve their outcomes or results continuously. The company makes each cell responsible for decisions on the resources that are most pertinent for achieving its objectives. For instance, the corporation may allow divisions to organize their regional structures differently. A significant amount of literature suggests that firms should limit autonomy or participative management and focus on organizing the work of the cells (self-management), as opposed to having cells set their own targets and organize their work (self-directed teams). Several studies suggest that cells that "self-set" their targets record higher levels of employee satisfaction, but not of performance, at least not at the team level.[9]

3. *Learning cycles*—Third, performance cells have periodic "reflection cycles," periods of learning when participants discuss new challenges, and leaders promote ruthless transparency and debate (using a dense information environment to address the mental biases of overoptimism and loss aversion). This is when people name the "elephants in the room" and solve problems jointly. Here, too, the solutions vary depending on the level at which performance cells are formed. In the case of a company or a large

business unit, the reflection and learning cycle may be longer, and could take place in the context of quarterly or monthly performance-review meetings. For smaller units such as lean teams, learning cycles may be shorter and could occur daily. Though the term "performance review" may suggest otherwise, the sessions are better used to reflect and learn collectively.

Inspired by the Kaizen concept at Toyota, many firms are creating more autonomous, self-managed teams within a large variety of functions. We nowadays often find them in functional divisions, such as sales, manufacturing, or back-office operations. These teams are often referred to as "lean teams."

An illustrative example of this is Whole Foods, an American firm founded in 1980 in Austin, Texas. Now the world's leader in natural and organic foods, it has more than 270 grocery stores in North America and the UK. The entire firm is organized as a set of self-managed teams. The teams are empowered to hire, fire, and allocate bonuses within their membership. Everyone is a key decision-maker, so everyone has access to all key business data. Information is shared so widely that the SEC considers all 36,000 employees as "insiders" for stock trading purposes.

*   *   *

Armed with a better understanding on how to design inspiration-driven transformations, let's see how James is doing at Influ. But before that, there is an unexpected crisis at home.

NOTES

1. C. A. Bartel and R. Saavedra, "The Collective Construction of Work Group Moods," *Administrative Science Quarterly* 45 (2000): 197–231.
2. T. Basford and B. Schaninger, "The Four Building Blocks of Change. Four Key Actions Influence Employee Mind-Sets and Behavior. Here's Why They Matter," *McKinsey Quarterly* (2016).

3. M. E. Gist, "Self-Efficacy: Implications for Organizational Behavior and Human Resource Management," *Academy of Management Review* 12, no. 3 (1987): 472–485.

4. Ibid.

5. M. Turner, *The Literary Mind: The Origins of Thought and Language* (New York: Oxford University Press, 1996).

6. A. Deutschman, "Change or Die. New Insights from Psychology and Neuroscience," *Fast Company* (2005).

7. C. Feser, *Serial Innovators. Firms that Change the World* (Hoboken, NJ: Wiley & Sons, 2011).

8. E. D. Beinhocker, *The Origin of Wealth: Evolution, Complexity, and the Radical Remaking of Economics* (Cambridge, MA: Harvard Business School Press, 2006).

9. A. Bandura, *Self-Efficacy: The Exercise of Control* (New York: W. H. Freeman, 1997).

CHAPTER 15

Influ—The Epilogue

On Sunday James takes the family out to a nice seafood dinner. When they get home, he and Joanne settle in the living room and become engrossed in a conversation about the problems James is facing at work.

Suddenly, they hear Elizabeth running down the stairs. She bursts into the room and interrupts them urgently, yelling, "Dad! Mummy! Come quick, something's really wrong with Max!" They dash upstairs to find that Max is breathing hard and starting to whimper. James immediately sees that the boy's face is turning red and swelling.

"Look at his arms, Dad," Elizabeth cries. "I was getting him a tube of skin cream at first because he was breaking out in itchy bumps, but then he started to breathe funny . . . so I came for you right away. What's wrong? What's wrong?"

"You did the right thing, honey," James tells her hurriedly. "But now we need to get him to a doctor immediately."

Terrified, but trying not to panic his daughter and his wife, James snatches Max up in his arms and runs out to the car. Elizabeth jumps in the back seat as Joanne cradles the boy in the front seat and calls the nearby hospital. James speeds to the emergency room. By the time they arrive, doctors are ready for Max. Quickly they examine him, finding that his oxygen levels are very low and noting that his other symptoms have worsened.

(continued)

(*continued*)

Doctors put Max—now sluggish and wheezing, his eyes swollen shut—on a gurney and trot with him through the double doors from the waiting room into the treatment area, with Joanne hurrying in their wake. The ER nurse explains to James and Elizabeth that only one visitor at a time can go back to the medical floor. She adds that the doctors think Max is having an episode of anaphylactic shock, probably an allergic reaction. She assures them that the ER team will immediately start medication, likely epinephrine, to stabilize the child and asks if they've ever been advised to carry an allergy medication injector with them at all times.

"No, no," James says, "He's always had some food allergies we've watched carefully, but nothing like this. . . ."

"He must have eaten something new or different, to have this kind of abrupt reaction," the nurse explains. "I'll go check on how he's doing, and I'll come out and let you know."

James puts his arm around Elizabeth, who is pale and shaking, and they sit down in the waiting room where every minute feels like an hour. They go over and over everything Max had for dinner, realizing that perhaps he'd never had shrimp before—because Joanne isn't so fond of it and doesn't serve it at home—and wondering if that could have been the trigger.

To their great relief, Joanne comes back into the waiting room before terribly long. "I have to get right back to Max," she says quickly, "but he's going to be okay. The medication made a tremendous difference right away. They may admit him overnight for observation, but I'll keep you posted. They said you could both come back and see him soon."

"I grabbed his blanket, Mom," Elizabeth says, handing Joanne a worn square of soft blue flannel.

"Good work, Liz," Joanne says, taking the faded blanket, her little soccer player's secret sleeping companion. "And you are one splendid big sister—you may have saved Max's life by letting us know so quickly what was going on. The doctor said we really were just in time with the epinephrine to avoid a really bad crisis. Children can die when this happens. We're going to have to keep an allergy injector on hand all the time from now on."

"I'll come back for you guys as soon as I can," she adds, walking away as the nurse admits her back through the ER's double doors.

"Don't you make things like that, Daddy?" Elizabeth asks.

"Things like what, honey?"

"Like those allergy shot things, those injectors that Max will need to carry now. I know a guy who's allergic to bee stings who keeps one with him all the time."

"That's a medical device, sweetheart. Influ has a subsidiary that makes hundreds of thousands of them."

"Maybe you could give some of them to school nurses," Elizabeth suggests. "Max needed it so fast . . . the school nurses are trained. They could save some kid's life."

"Maybe we could, sweetie," James replies choking up. "Maybe we could."

And suddenly, he remembers why working at Influ really matters.

* * *

For James, who now and forever sees himself as the father of a son who narrowly escaped death, helping people is very important, even more than it was before. The three business-unit heads, for their own reasons and despite their different backgrounds, all have one thing in common: they share a strong desire to help people live better lives. That's the very reason they joined Influ in the first place and have stayed with it, through ups and downs, mostly downs.

He decides to appeal to the value that they all share—all three business unit heads and himself.

He knows he has to tell them about Max.

(continued)

(*continued*)

He invites the three unit heads to an off-site location to discuss how to take the company forward.

James wants to talk to them about his plans for Influ. He explains from his heart that he wants to refocus Influ on what it originally stood for: not profits and efficiency, but rather, helping people live better lives and making the world better.

"With our products we can help people live better and stay well. There are still large areas of unmet diagnostic and medical needs. We will tap into them. That's what we will focus on, and that's what we will invest in. I'm sure that profits will eventually follow, but I don't want to run the company with the sole objective of maximizing the money," James says, bracing himself to reveal his own emotions, but wishing for their support, and even hoping to regain their trust.

"We can make this company mean something, refocus it on having a mission, on saving lives and improving the world," he says, noticing that Jorg is watching him intently.

"We almost lost our son, our eight-year-old, a couple of weeks ago to an episode of anaphylaxis, a sudden allergic reaction, shock," James begins, trying not to tear up. He hears Mary gasp. "What saved his life was his sister's fast reaction to his symptoms—so we got him to the ER immediately and got a dose of epinephrine onboard fast enough. Now, we keep an auto-injector in his backpack, in the car, in the kitchen, and in his bedroom. These are Influ auto-injectors, from one of Jorg's subsidiaries. I've asked our corporate responsibility people to look into doing a whole program to donate auto-injectors to schools for their nurses to have on hand. That was my daughter's idea, but she showed me, this idea shows us, the kind of company we can be, and the kind of things we can do—if you're with me."

Then, spent, he waits to see what they will say. He expects some cynicism, some resistance, given the unit heads' long patience, but he doesn't get either reaction.

On the contrary, they immediately express their relief that Max is doing well. Jorg takes a deep breath, thinking of his nearly faded hope that he can help cancer patients like his late wife through his work at Influ. Mary stands up and comes over to James to give him an unprecedented quick hug, quietly giving thanks for her four strong sons. And Quentin clasps James' hand and congratulates him on Max's quick recovery. "No more shrimp for our boy," Quentin says, trying to sound hearty so he doesn't reveal how touched he is, "quite enough of that!"

Max's story prompts the three division heads to share their own life stories.

The members of Influ's top team wrap up their personal accounts—Jorg's loss of his first wife and his resulting change of profession; Mary's struggles as a woman, a wife, and mother, in her father's world, a man's world, of professional scientific research; and Quentin's transition from his youthful hopes of becoming a professional competitive skier into success in the world of business, where he's had to try hard to learn to be more likeable—as a group of colleagues who really care for one another.

As they listen to each other, they each find that in their private thoughts, they're making important personal decisions emerging from their new sense of commitment to Influ. Always a reserved man, Jorg realizes how deep his love and gratitude are for Ilsa, his second wife. He knows he'll have to swallow his usual emotional restraint and tell her that he cherishes her all the more for her support in fighting cancer in their volunteer work together and in his professional quest.

Mary decides once and for all to tell the American colleagues who've been trying to hire her for their big New England pharmaceutical company that she's staying in London with Influ. She knows her husband and the lads will be relieved, and that's part of the joy she feels.

Quentin decides to propose to Chloe, his long-time girlfriend. "This is my life," he thinks, "I'm not that kid on the slopes anymore. What am I waiting for?"

(continued)

(*continued*)

Their emotional, touching autobiographical stories give them deep insights into one another's feelings, wishes, dreams, anxieties, motivations, and frustrations. The process of telling each other their personal sagas has an unexpected side effect: It increases their mutual trust and collegial warmth.

After listening to all the stories, James sits back, and says, "So let's save some lives."

James' fresh energy, engagement, and purposeful sense of mission ignite the spark that drives a new attitude at Influ. His personal experience with his children helps him bring his values alive. His touching story shows his team that James is more than a CEO; he's a loving and caring father, and given Max's quick recovery, overall his story is uplifting and very pertinent to Influ's future.

* * *

Then the four of them start to brainstorm about what it will take to get Influ back into the business of helping people heal. They speak about the need for a full corporate transformation and jointly define an ambitious set of actions and a more patient-oriented plan for the future. Suddenly, their frustration, anger, and negative emotions seem to have dissipated. Their sense of being a leadership team, their excitement, positive energy, willingness to collaborate, and collective commitment to Influ are back.

James is still concerned that the positive impact of this change in his leadership approach could wear off after a few months, especially if setbacks occur in the course of the transformation. After all, hasn't he gone through this once already? Influ needs a lot of work.

He knows that using soft influencing with an emphasis on empathetic engagement may lead to increased commitment, but real business results have to emerge. He mentally reviews his latest conversations with Marc, when they decided to augment his inspirational appeals with additional soft influencing approaches tailored to the specific, most salient characteristics of each business unit head.

Mary's salient feature is her openness to James' ideas and arguments, and her hope that he can help her attract big-name scientists. James knows he can be open and direct in trying to influence Mary. He turns to rational persuasion, the most straightforward influencing tactic. James uses logic and concrete assurances to reinforce his appeal to Mary's values. "I share your urgency about innovating," he tells her, "and I've identified two companies we could buy, one in Switzerland and one in the US, to deepen our innovation capabilities."

Quentin's salient emotional feature—as with Carl, the chairman—is his emotional predisposition to feelings of anger, particularly when things aren't going well in his division. People who experience anger more than others tend to be action-oriented, ambitious competitive risk takers. They sometimes tend to see the world as a battlefield, categorizing others as enemies or friends ("black and white"), and to personalize conflicts. James decides to arouse Quentin's anger by refocusing him on beating his Asian competitors, not just one Japanese firm, but all of them ("They are making inroads and attacking you") and offering support ("I am on your side. How can I best support you in this competition?").

Jorg's salient feature is conscientiousness. Conscientious people tend to be good targets for ingratiation and other socializing tactics. Ingratiation entails telling someone that he or she has special skills or qualifications and praising past performance. That's exactly what James does. ("Your help was instrumental before and during the turnaround. It made a real difference. I've relied heavily on your friendship.")

Over time, these interventions work, and the unit heads sustain their excitement about change and their dedication to

(continued)

(*continued*)

making it work. They energize their divisions and make the most of the company's renewed commitment to investing in the equipment and personnel they need.

But James and his division heads don't stop there. James hands out Marc Jansen's notes on inspiration-based company transformations. After his colleagues read the papers, they discuss and debate them. They conclude that they need to launch a corporation-wide change program based on the four elements of the Influence Model.

- First, they jointly develop a change story around the concept of "helping people live better lives." They do not run surveys about culture or values; they follow what they think is right based on their experience and their emotions. They feel strongly that this is the perfect mission for Influ and they are confident that it will appeal to most of the people in the organization. And if some of them just don't get it, maybe Influ isn't the right place for them.

- Second, they agree to be role models of the values embedded in the corporate change stories. It isn't very difficult. After all, they are doing what they really believe in; they are being totally authentic. They also agree that they will explicitly challenge one another, should anyone not take action according to these common values. That applies to everyone, including James.

- Third, James decides to change Influ's planning and performance management system to empower the business unit heads. Strategic plans and decisions on business initiatives won't remain his lone responsibility, even with the help of Jane Cunningham's strategy department. James plans to focus on setting targets and coaching the business-unit heads, as he lets them become accountable for developing and implementing their own plans. He also encourages them to share in the research and resources offered by the strategy, admin and finance departments. This is a huge change, not so much for Jane Cunningham, who has broad collaborative experience, or for Jorg, who worked in a similar system at his former employer, the car manufacturer, but for Mary and Quentin. As the two "Influ veterans" on the top team, they're used to top-down leadership. They've never had any experience with being independent leaders or working as part of a self-managed team, and neither have most of their subordinates.

■ Fourth, they jointly launch a leadership development program for Influ's top 100 potential future leaders, 25 from each division, and 25 from finance, strategy, and administration. It is clear to each of them that moving to a system of "self-managed" performance cells requires giving up-and-coming leaders a different set of skills. Now, executives and managers will be accountable for their own plans and results, so their training must focus on building competencies in solving problems, developing strategic plans, and setting priorities.

Only a few months later Influ is aflame with positive energy. These changes affect the entire organization very quickly. Like a brush fire, excitement and enthusiasm for new initiatives and rededication to Influ's products spread through the organization.

Things are changing fast, and for real this time. Influ's innovation pipeline quickly fills up. Sales improve, and after a few months, the company starts to grow. As evidence of exceptionally strong growth mounts, Carl calls James in to tell him that any discussion of selling Influ is off the table.

Instead, Carl, James, the board, and the management team are now discussing big acquisitions. . . .

* * *

Afterword

"Inspirational leadership helps people grow—not just a few, but thousands, and sometimes millions of people."

A true leader is a person whose influence inspires people to do what is expected of them to do. You cease to be a leader when you manipulate with your ego instead of convincing by your inspiration.

—Israelmore Ayivor

In this short book we reviewed the strategy of leading by inspiring others. This is the most powerful approach to creating commitment, passion, energy, persistence, and innovation in organizations because it addresses the way people learn and develop at the neuronal level. Inspirational leadership accelerates behavioral and organizational change because it builds on the very mechanisms the human brain uses to learn and to change itself. We saw that applying inspirational leadership is the most effective approach in complex and dynamic situations, and in situations in which people are "emotional," that is, under pressure and stressed, such as when an organization is going through a transformation process.

Inspirational leadership accelerates change at scale. In fact, it is probably the only leadership approach based on soft influencing tactics that leaders can apply at scale. Rational persuasion is rather ineffective; socializing, exchanging, personal appeals, and consultation are effective influencing approaches, but are hard to scale. How do you ask a favor of 10,000 people in an organization? How do you use exchange or consultation in an organization that's active in dozens of countries?

However, you can apply inspirational leadership approaches to lead change in an organizational unit, in a company, in an industry, in a country, or in the world. Think of inspirational leaders like John F. Kennedy, Mahatma Gandhi, or Nelson Mandela. Inspirational leadership may actually be the only viable leadership approach that can steer large organizations to survive and thrive for longer periods of time in today's dynamic markets; it may be the only approach that enables companies to battle the winds of creative destruction successfully over long periods of time.

In Parts Two and Three we discussed frameworks and methods that might be useful as a starting point for building competence and confidence in using inspirational leadership. Part Three and Four provide the "toolbox" you will need to exercise leadership through inspiration.

One question remains: should *you* apply the tools in the toolbox?

There are two angles to this question.

First, you can use inspirational leadership to manipulate others. By appealing to their values and arousing their emotions, you can direct people and get them to do as you wish. Importantly, an inspiring leader can get others to do things that may not be in their best interests, but only serve the leader. For instance, a company leader may launch a cost-reduction program and ask all the firm's employees to accept a pay cut for the sake of a greater good, like making the company stronger and more competitive, and securing their employment. In so doing, the leader may appeal to such values as helping others ("by accepting a pay cut, you will save jobs") and fairness ("we are all taking a pay cut"). The leader could even make this appeal while hiding the fact that lower costs and improved results will mean that he or she earns a hefty bonus at the end of the year. Or, for instance, a political leader may arouse voters' frustration and anger to win an election, but then not care about implementing good governance.

Manipulative inspirational leadership may get people to accept a pay cut and may help win an election, but it is a short-lived approach. When the information that the company leader is not taking a pay cut personally becomes public, the influencing approach will fail, and will create organizational cynicism, resentment, and resistance.

Or, when the political leader fails to implement promised changes
for the public good, the citizenry may protest, perhaps even violently,
and vote the scoundrel out of office at the next election.

For inspirational leadership to be effective and not manipulative,
the leader must be authentic and "walk the talk." Being authentic
means truly caring for those whose emotions you are arousing, and
being prepared to do what you are asking others to do. In short,
if you don't care about others—their values and their emotions—
then you don't really care about inspiring them and you shouldn't
try inspirational leadership under false pretenses. The backlash is too
damaging.

Second, inspirational leadership implies empowering others.
"Igniting" others—creating commitment, passion, enthusiasm,
energy—is useless if those being inspired do not have the ability to
affect change. For inspirational leadership to work, the leader must
empower others so they can make change happen. Some leaders feel
uncomfortable delegating power, feeling that they are losing control,
such as when a CEO releases his or her power to decide on head-
counts centrally, and delegates the decisions on managing headcount
to several business unit leaders. "What if one or two of them get it
wrong? What if they all get it wrong?" the leader may say. Inspirational leadership implicitly includes understanding others' capabilities, strengths, and weaknesses, and delegating power appropriately.
It implies being confident and trusting others. A leader who isn't
confident and does not trust others can't exercise inspirational
leadership. It won't work.

But leaders who care about those they lead, and trust them, will
find that inspirational leadership can help them make a difference to
the world.

Authentic, entrusting inspirational leadership doesn't exploit
people—it develops them. Inspired people are committed, passionate, energized, and empowered. They take initiatives, make decisions,
innovate, and create; by doing so, they learn, develop confidence, and
grow as individuals, in the workplace and well beyond. Our brain is
naturally wired to learn; it is eager to make new synaptic connections
and to progress. Inspirational leadership harnesses the brain's natural

eagerness to learn and grow, and makes it happen. By inspiring others, a leader can develop their minds and their futures. This form of leadership can help people grow—not just a few, but thousands, and sometimes millions of people.

By helping people grow, become more confident, more creative, and more effective, a leader can make a difference in life—to individual people, to groups of people, to organizations, to nations, and to the world.

Appendix I: Leadership Behaviors

Based on our experience and the review of academic literature we identified 20 leadership behaviors, which we tested for their power to predict variances in organizational health.

The 20 leadership behaviors are:

- Be supportive
- Champion desired change
- Clarify objectives, rewards, and consequences
- Communicate prolifically and enthusiastically
- Develop others
- Develop and share a collective mission
- Differentiate among followers
- Facilitate group collaboration
- Foster mutual respect
- Give praise
- Keep the group organized on task
- Make quality decisions
- Motivate and bring out the best in others
- Offer a critical perspective
- Operate with a strong result orientation
- Recover positively from failures
- Remain composed and confident in uncertainty
- Role model organizational values
- Seek different perspectives
- Solve problems effectively

Appendix II: Organizational Health Index

McKinsey's Organizational Health Index (OHI) measures an organization's health along two dimensions: observable health outcomes and supporting management practices. Health outcomes describe how staff "experience" the organization's health (because of, or in spite of, practices). Management practices measure the frequency with which an organization exercises behaviors to achieve goals. An analogy that may be helpful: outcomes represent a patient's health (e.g., blood pressure), and practices represent behaviors (e.g., diet, exercise)

There are nine observable health outcomes, and 37 practices measured in the OHI:

1. *Direction*: The extent to which there is a clear sense of where the organization is heading and how it will get there that is meaningful to all employees. Three practices drive the direction health outcome:
   - Shared vision
   - Strategic clarity
   - Employee involvement
2. *Leadership*: The extent to which leaders inspire actions by others. The practices are:
   - Authoritative leadership
   - Consultative leadership
   - Supportive leadership
   - Challenging leadership
3. *Culture and climate*: The shared beliefs and quality of interactions within and across organizational units. The practices are:
   - Open and trusting
   - Internally competitive
   - Operationally disciplined
   - Creative and entrepreneurial

4. *Accountability*: The extent to which individuals understand what is expected of them, have authority, and take responsibility for delivering results. The practices are:
   - Role clarity
   - Performance contracts
   - Consequence management
   - Personal ownership

5. *Coordination and control*: The ability to evaluate organizational performance and risk, and to address issues and opportunities when they arise. The practices are:
   - People performance review
   - Operational management
   - Financial management
   - Professional standards
   - Risk management

6. *Capabilities*: The presence of the institutional skills and talent required to execute strategy and create competitive advantage. The practices are:
   - Talent acquisition
   - Talent development
   - Process-based capabilities
   - Outsourced expertise

7. *Motivation*: The presence of enthusiasm that drives employees to put in extraordinary effort to deliver results. The practices are:
   - Meaningful values
   - Inspirational leaders
   - Career opportunities
   - Financial incentives
   - Rewards and recognition

8. *External orientation*: The quality of engagement with customers, suppliers, partners and other external stakeholders to drive value. The practices are:
   - Customer focus
   - Competitive insights
   - Business partnerships
   - Government and community relations

9. *Innovation and learning*: The quality and flow of new ideas and the ability to adapt and shape the organization as needed. The practices are:
 ▪ Top-down innovation
 ▪ Bottom-up innovation
 ▪ Knowledge sharing
 ▪ Capturing external ideas

The scores of the outcomes are combined to calculate the OHI score. The OHI score is a strong predictor of shareholder returns.[1]

NOTES

1. A. De Smet, B. Schaninger, and M. Smith, "The Hidden Value of Organizational Health—And How to Capture It," *McKinsey Quarterly* (2014).

Appendix III: Personality Markers

Dimension	Open	Conscientious	Extrovert	Agreeable	Neurotic
Description	Are open to experience; are intellectually curious, appreciative of art and sensitive to beauty; tend to be creative and aware of their feelings; are more likely to hold unconventional beliefs; are able to think in symbols and abstractions far removed from concrete experience; are rather progressive (as opposed to conservative)	Have a tendency to show self-discipline; act dutifully; aim for achievement against measurements or beyond expectations; prefer planned action; appear more structured	Enjoy being with people; are often perceived as full of energy; tend to be enthusiastic, action-oriented; are likely to talk, assert themselves, and draw attention to themselves	Value getting along with others; are considerate, friendly, generous, helpful, and willing to compromise their interests with others; are good team players; have an optimistic view of human nature	Are emotionally reactive and vulnerable to stress; are more likely to interpret ordinary situations as threatening or frustrating; their negative emotional reactions tend to persist for unusually long periods of time; have a diminished ability to think clearly, make decisions, and cope with stress; lack contentment

(continued)

Dimension	Open	Conscientious	Extrovert	Agreeable	Neurotic
Top 10 markers of behavior	1. Have a rich vocabulary	1. Are always prepared	1. Are the life of the party	1. Are interested in people	1. Are not relaxed most of the time
	2. Have a vivid imagination	2. Pay attention to details	2. Feel comfortable around people	2. Sympathize with others' feelings	2. Often feel blue
	3. Have excellent ideas	3. Get chores done right away	3. Start conversations	3. Have a soft heart	3. Get stressed out easily
	4. Are quick to understand things	4. Like order	4. Talk to a lot of different people at parties	4. Take time out for others	4. Worry about things
	5. Use difficult words	5. Follow a schedule	5. Don't mind being the center of attention	5. Feel others' emotions	5. Are easily disturbed
	6. Spend time reflecting on things	6. Are exacting in their work	6. Talk a lot	6. Make people feel at ease	6. Get upset easily
	7. Are full of ideas	7. Do not leave their belongings strewn around	7. Do not stay in the background	7. Are interested in others	7. Change their mood a lot
	8. Do not have difficulty understanding abstract ideas	8. Do not make a mess of things	8. Have a lot to say	8. Do not insult people	8. Have frequent mood swings
	9. Are interested in abstract ideas	9. Do not often forget to put things back in their place	9. Like to draw attention to themselves	9. Are interested in other people's problems	9. Get irritated easily
	10. Have a good imagination	10. Do not shirk their duties	10. Are not quiet around strangers	10. Feel concern for others	10. Often feel blue

Source: "International Personality Item Tool" from R. R. McCrae and O. P. John, "An Introduction to the Five-Factor Model and Its Applications," *Journal of Personality* 60, no. 2 (1992): 175–215.

Appendix IV: Emotional Disposition Markers

Dimension	Anxiety	Anger	Sadness
Description	Tend to be very collaborative; tend to be good at reading others; tend to be good at navigating complex social situations (always "scanning" the environment); tend to be able to develop enormous amount of energy, especially to address any anxieties they may have ("insecure overachiever"); tend to be rather shy and timid; tend to dislike confrontations (and are therefore at times perceived as being "political" and smooth); tend to be risk-averse; like to share responsibilities	Tend to be ambitious; tend to take action; tend to be risk-takers, entrepreneurs, and people who build things; tend to enjoy competition and productive confrontations; tend to see the world as a battlefield or a competition; tend to categorize others in enemies and friends ("black and white"); tend to personalize conflicts; blue and yellow people tend to feel threatened in their presence	Tend to be very agreeable; tend to display a high level of empathy, tend to be very collaborative. Tend to have a low level of energy; may be rather melancholic and pessimistic, attracting empathy and support; may enjoy the experience of sadness
Typical markers of behavior	Don't make decisions easily. Build committees/ seek group support in decisions. Politically astute/ smooth.	Are ambitious, visionary, bold. Make decisions fast. Build teams (of followers), build "things." Value loyalty.	Have a low level of energy. Are pessimistic. Are good at sensing others.

Source: P. Ekman, *Emotions Revealed: Recognizing Faces and Feelings to Improve Communication and Emotional Life* (New York: St. John's Press, 2007); C. Feser and P. Gurdjian, "Growing Leaders. A Light-Hearted Introduction to Leadership Development." McKinsey internal publication, 2014.

Acknowledgments

Numerous people have contributed to this short book with their ideas, observations, and suggestions. All mistakes in the book are no doubt mine.

I would like to thank the following individuals (in alphabetical order): Zafer Achi, Asa Bjornberg, Aaron de Smet, Pierre Gurdjian, Thomas Halbeisen, Neil Janin, Robert Kegan, Lisa Lahey, Mary Meaney, Erica Meyer Rauzin, Michael Rennie, Julia Sperling, Nick van Dam, Graham Ward, Allen Webb, Charles Whitehouse, and Emily Yeah.

About the Author

Claudio Feser is a Senior Partner in the Zurich office of McKinsey & Company.

He is the leader of McKinsey Academy, a practice of the firm that focuses on helping organizations develop leaders (www.mckinsey.com/mckinseyacademy).

Prior to leading McKinsey Academy, between 1999 and 2004 he built and led the Greece office, and between 2004 and 2010 he led the Switzerland office of McKinsey & Company.

Claudio is the author or co-author of several articles including "Long Live Bureaucracy! A More Nuanced Perspective on Hierarchies" published by Jossey-Bass in *Leader to Leader* in 2012, "Decoding Leadership" published by *McKinsey Quarterly* in 2014, and "Guidelines for Selecting a Departmental Chair of Medicine" published by *Nature* (online) in 2015.

He is the author of the book *Serial Innovators: Firms That Change the World*, published by John Wiley & Sons in 2011.

Claudio lives in Zurich. He is married and father of two sons.

Index